Dowsed Treasure Locations Around The World

By Aquila Chrysaestos

Published by New Generation Publishing in 2017

Copyright © Aquila Chrysaestos 2017

First Edition

The author asserts the moral right under the Copyright, Designs and Patents Act 1988 to be identified as the author of this work.

All Rights reserved. No part of this publication may be reproduced, stored in a retrieval system or transmitted, in any form or by any means without the prior consent of the author, nor be otherwise circulated in any form of binding or cover other than that which it is published and without a similar condition being imposed on the subsequent purchaser.

Information available in the book provided "as is". The author makes no representations or warranties either expressed or implied as to the accuracy of the information in these pages or its fitness for any purpose whatsoever. The author cannot be held responsible for any loss, accident, injury, or death which may occur from any reader's misunderstanding or modifying published data in this book.

The author makes no representations or warranties either expressed or implied as to the accuracy of the information given by manufactures of products listed on featured website links listed in this book. The author does not have any commercial connection with any of these companies, and has supplied data to encourage you the reader to research into new and modern treasure hunting techniques, and seek out new technologies that will speed up treasure detection when carrying out your own field operations. The author is not trying to promote new products or suggest that the reader should purchase any of these items shown on the following featured pages of this book.

www.newgeneration-publishing.com

My many thanks go to Miss Georgia Dunn for editing the book cover, Mr David Villanueva and Mr J.P.Taylor for helping me proof read and edit this book for publication, and supplying me with their vast dowsing experiences and site photographs taken at dowsed sites in England and in Dubai.

For You Josh Love Dad xx

Contents

1. Introduction 1
2. Dowsing and the Sceptics 4
3. Your Plan Of Action For A Successful Treasure Recovery 16
4. Finding Buried Treasure 19
5. Does Buried Gold Give Off An Aura? 22

European Treasure Locations

6. Nazi Treasure Lake Toplitz Austria.. 27
7. Lake Lünersee Nazi Treasure Locations Austria 34
8. More SS Nazi War Treasure Alt Aussee Region of Austria............ 36
9. Waltham Abbey Treasure England.. 39
10. Capt. Avery Treasure, Cornwall, England 45
11. The Merchant Royal Wreck Cornwall, England 46
12. King John's Lost Treasure, The Wash England............................. 47
13. Loch Arkaig Treasure Locations Scotland...................................60
14. The Treasure of Largo Law Scotland 63
15. The Royal Charter Ship Wreck, Anglesey Wales 65
16. Rennes-le-Château Treasure in France.. 70
17. Lost Nazi Treasure Locations in Deutschneudorf Germany............ 72
18. HMS Frigate Lutine, Vlieland Northern Holland 75
19. Monte Sorrate Nazi Treasure in Italy 83
20. Adolf Hitler's Wolf's Liar Treasure in Poland................................ 84
21. The Zbiroh Castle Nazi Hidden Treasure in the Czech Republic.... 89

USA and Canada Treasure Locations

22. Superstitions Mountains Lost Dutchman Gold Mine Location Arizona USA 93
23. Locations of the Spanish Fleet 1553-4 Texas USA 101
24. Poverty Island Treasure, Lake Mitchigan USA 107
25. The Alamo Mission San Antonio Texas Treasure USA 108
26. Atocha & Margarita Wreck Sites Key West Florida USA 112
27. Oak Island Treasure Locations Nova Scotia, Canada 115

Asian Treasure Locations

28. Yamashita Treasure Locations in the Philippines 119
29. The Awa Maru Treasure Ship in the Philippines...................... 125
30. The Flor Do Mar Treasure Ship Location Malacca Straits, Malaysia 137

31.	"The Dolphin Wreck" Sri Lanka	138
32.	Genghis Khan Tomb and Treasure in Mongolia	139

Egypt Treasure Locations

33.	Red Sea Treasure Ship Wreck Locations in the Red Sea Egypt	143
34.	The Ancient City of Tanis Treasure Location Egypt	144

Other Treasure Locations

35.	The Treasure Locations on Cocos Island	146
36.	Island Of Dominica Spanish Fleet Location	148
37.	Conclusion	149

Bibliography	150
Appendix	151

1. Introduction

Following on from my first book entitled: General Yamashita's Dream Book: How To Successfully Find Treasure In The Philippines by Aquila Chrysaetos (**ISBN 978-1-909740-29-7** www.Amazon.com)

I have decided to compile my second book based upon my experiences of dowsing for lost treasure from around the world using the same dowsing techniques that I have learnt from the famous paranormal dowser and author Mr Uri Geller.

In his book: Uri Geller's Crystal Pendulum Dowsing Kit: Find Wealth, Health and Well-Being by Dowsing and Divining, (**ISBN-13: 978-1842931943**) Uri Geller explains how all of us have the dowsing gift he says:

"All of us have the instinctive power of our intuition, but in this modern world, we have become disconnected from this ancient art. Uri Geller is famous around the world for his paranormal skills. In this amazing kit, he guides you step by step into the hidden world of dowsing. The box includes: a crystal pendulum - the essential tool for successful dowsing; a pair of divining rods - used by dowsers for thousands of years to locate water, oil, or precious objects buried underground; and "Learn How to Dowse Guide" - A fun, practical book which explains dowsing techniques in detail. This kit teaches you basic skills you need to dowse using a crystal pendulum or divining rods. It then explains how to use these skills to find lost objects, water, fossils, oil, treasures and archaeological remains. Uri Geller reveals how dowsing can help you on the path to success, health and happiness".

Using the knowledge I have learnt from this book, and developing my own technique to find gold auras using a gold ring to tune into the energy of gold and dowsing maps, I found that I could feel the presence of gold in the centre of the palm of my right hand. When my hand was over the gold I could feel a "hot spot" in the centre of my right palm indicating the presence of the gold at that location on the map or photograph. While in my left hand I held my solid gold ring.
By tuning into the resonant frequency or energy from the item you are looking for. You are tuning in just like a radio receiver into the object you are seeking.

Many dowsers will use a small sample of the material they want to find, this could be gold, silver, copper, diamond, or sweet water for drinking or even oil. Whatever you are seeking it can be found through training and practice.

Over the past 12 years I have dowsed Google Earth™ looking for such "Gold Hot Spots" and recorded my findings using the "yellow Add Place mark" function found on the top left side menu found on Google Earth™ software package. I have helped many Filipino treasure hunters find hidden Japanese Imperial treasure buried in the Philippines, and dowsed a site near to General Santos in 2006 where the owner found a 55 gallon oil drum buried at a depth of 21 feet containing forty four 6.2Kg bars of gold. I have identified gold by using the term "Au" **to represent Gold** which is the international symbol **"Au"** (from the Latin term: *aurum*) and the atomic number of 79.

The Philippines and many other places in the world hold many billions of dollars worth of lost treasure, whether it be buried on land or lost in the depths of Lakes and Oceans.

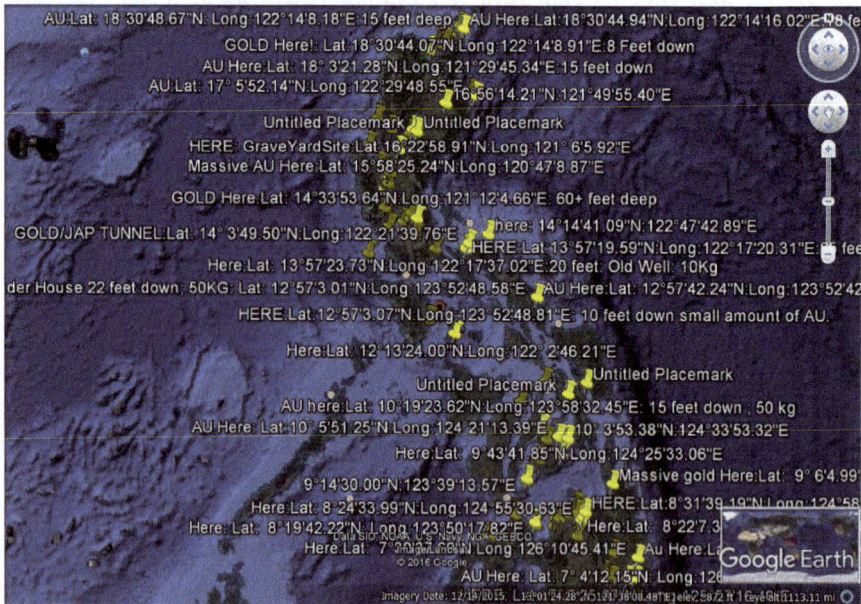

Here is an example of my dowsing activities over the past decade, the picture above shows the Philippines and the GPS locations of many deposits of gold dowsed for many Filipino treasure hunters. This map is awash of treasure locations buried by the Japanese Imperial Army and also

2

includes natural gold deposits. My dowsing activities have not been limited to just SE Asia as you will see in this book. Some readers will ask the question, why give the treasure locations away to complete strangers when I could have recovered them myself. The answer to this question is simple: I do not have the time or the financial means to travel and recover these lost treasures from around the world. I believe I would have to have ten life times to recover the billions of dollars worth of treasure awaiting discovery. I feel that if other like-minded treasure hunters should now progress my research to a successful conclusion then so much the better. I will concentrate my efforts on "treasures of my own that require planning and funding. These projects include:

Description of Recovery Project in UK and Abroad	Dowsed & Verified Target Value UK Pounds (Million)	Status & Funding (UK Pounds)
Spitfire Seaplane in Lake (only 6 made last one intact)	Yes Have GPS Location Have Recovery Plan (£2M)	Active require £80K To extract from lake
840 Rolls Royce Merlin Aero Engines in Crates buried 1945	Yes GPS and detected location myself (3-5M)	To dig £35K Have buyers
King Johns Treasure The Wash, Lincs. (UK)	Yes Have GPS Location (£2-4 M)	Will verify in Aug. 2017 Require £180K to dig
Ballot Island Gold Bullion The Philippines	Yes Have GPS location (£8M)	To Verify & Detect (£8K) Recovery plan to follow
Japanese Shinto Shrine Buddha and 75Kg gold bars, Luzon	Yes Have GPS Location And funded digging (£10M)	Requires extra Funding (£280K next visit May 2017)

In this book I write about the history of the lost treasure, and give a dowsed location of where I have sensed the gold aura is coming from. I show you the location using Google Earth Maps and the GPS reference of the target(s) in question. The accuracy of the target is as near to the place as I can get, and maybe up to 4-10 metres away. I have done the donkey work for you, all you have do is verify my findings through a little more research and on site ground work, then make a plan to recover the treasure for yourself.

2. Dowsing and the Sceptics

In this book I will not be explaining how to use a Pendulum or how to dowse using dividing rods. I will however strongly suggest that you invest in one of many books available on the market that explains how to dowse. One such book written by a fellow treasure hunter and a dowser called David Villanueva who lives in England, explains the process and technique of dowsing very well. The book is called Dowsing for Treasure, The New Successful Treasure Hunter's Essential Dowsing Manual (ISBN 9781518766060) available through True Treasure Books (**www.truetreasurebooks.net**).

There are many sceptics that are out there who believe that dowsing cannot work simply because it has no scientific theory that can be proved in a way that they understand. To these people who are not open minded to an ancient art that has been practiced by thousands of dowsers long before Christ was on the earth, I say open your closed minds and listen up you may learn something that may be of value to you later on in your life!

This book is my collection of dowsed targets that require further investigation and recovery by those who have an open mind and will look at my findings in a positive way.

Dowsers are not full of ego, or want to be famous for having a God given gift to dowse. These people are not seeking celebrity on social media or on some mindless celebrity TV show. They are normal people who want to help humanity in some way. Dowsing does not work if your questions are motivated by greed. The proper intent and the need to ask for permission to dowse for an object and the motivation behind the questions are more important and crucial to receiving accurate answers and continued success.

According to the Toronto Dowsers in Canada:
"Critics of dowsing claim it is not accurate. The dowsing system is accurate, all you need is to ask the right question, have the right intent, focus and concentration. To receive an accurate response you cannot force or influence the pendulum. This is part of the learning and the practice. At a recent meeting when we were told that good dowsers have an accuracy rate of 86%."

"Dowsing has been difficult to explain scientifically, not because it is not scientific because it is highly scientific, it is our "science" which is backward and not well advanced as it has not yet developed the tools by which it can observe and measure what is going on when a dowser uses his or her ability to dowse. To me everything on this planet has an energy field, as a dowser I tune into this energy to locate what I am seeking. It is really that simple. It is individuals that over think and complicate the dowsing process.

Dowsing is accepted and practiced by more and more people including medical practitioners, simply because it works, and its results are verified, largely because linear and time consuming studies come to the same conclusions. This is a powerful art that ought to be approached and appreciated with respect and with knowledge.

Dowsers from around the world every day use the art of dowsing to carry out hundreds of activities that science **CANNOT** solve. Where the science ends dowsing may have the answer for the 21st century and beyond.

Here is a practical list showing how a dowser can help his community and industry when science has failed to give positive answers to unanswered questions, whether in the past, present or the future.

To Find Oil and Water

Professor Hans Dieter Betz (professor of physics, Munich University) headed a team of scientists that investigated the ability of dowsers to find underground drinkable supplies, taking them to 10 different countries and, on the advice of dowers, sank some 2,000 wells with a very high success rate. In Sri Lanka, where the geological conditions are said to be difficult, some 691 wells were drilled for, based on the advice of dowsers, with a **96%** success rate. Geohydrologists given the same task took two months to evaluate a site where a dowser would complete his survey in minutes. The geohydrologists had a measly **21%** success rate, as a result of which the German government has sponsored 100 dowers to work in the arid zones of Southern India to find drinkable water.

Evelyn Penrose: A noted dowser Evelyn Penrose was retained by British Columbia to locate oil and water resources. During 1931-1932 she also located 392 water wells for homesteaders.
    (See: http://www.denverspiritualcommunity.org/Dowsing.htm).

Emmy Kittemann: Daughter of a dowser was one of the most acclaimed dowsers in Germany. In her most famous case, she correctly dowsed the location of a mineralized spring for the village of Tegernsee. All previous drillings found only water with heavy sulfur content. Yet Kitteman accurately predicted the depth at which the water would be found as well as its iodine-rich content.

"U.S Army General Patton had a complete willow tree flown to Morocco so that two young men from Tennessee transferred to his unit could use the willow branches to dowse to find water to replace the wells the German Army had blown up during WWII".
(Quoted from Don Nolan in his article A Brief History of Dowsing).

To Help With Unsolved Murders

In 17th century France, Messr Jacques Aymar Vernay, a stonemason by trade, used his dowsing talents to successfully track criminals. His dowsing rod, on more than one occasion, led authorities to the whereabouts of murderers.
(See: http://archive.randi.org/site/index.php/swift-blog/2320-dowsing-for-murder.html)

To Locate a Lost Dog

In December, 1992, Mr. and Mrs. Anders and Berith Lindgren were hunting with their friends when their dog ran off and disappeared. An extensive search proved fruitless. A few days later they sought the help of dowser Leif Andersson. His dowsing techniques led the hunters to a small lake where they indeed found the body of the dog, where it had apparently fallen through the thin ice and died.

To Locate Land Mines During Conflicts

During The Vietnam War (1st of November 1955 to 30th of April 1975): The 1st and 3rd U.S. Marine Divisions in Vietnam used dowsing as a simple, low-cost method for locating Vietcong tunnels, which were used for communication, storage depots, supply network, command posts, training centres, hospitals, land mines and sally ports for over twenty years.

(Bossart 1968 in the Project *Poorboy* Annual Progress Report; Bird 1979, Chapter 11). Mr Louis Maticia, was the dowser who ran the program and taught the Marines to dowse. In the Falklands war (2nd April to 14th June 1982): The British Army used dowsers on the Falkland Islands to locate land mines.

To Locate Lost People in WWII Bomb Craters

During the Second World War, England's Warwickshire Police Force secretly used one of its own officers who was skilled at dowsing was asked to try and locate the bodies of two local men lost in one of many bomb craters made by the German bombers the night before. Mr James Hiatt and Mr Harry Marston had been buried and feared dead under the soil and rubble of one of several massive bomb craters made by the Nazi attackers.

A classified report dated July 1941 and filed by a Sergeant J. Hall of Warwickshire Police stated: *"I was at the scene when I noticed P.C. 319 Terry coming from a nearby thicket fashioning a forked stick with a penknife. P.C. Terry commenced to walk over the bomb craters. About 30 seconds later he came to a standstill and I noticed that the forked stick which he was holding had commenced to wriggle very violently and he had great difficulty in holding it. He pointed to a particular portion of heaped soil near to one of the craters and said: 'They are under there.'"*

Sergeant Hall added: *"A quarter of an hour later the bodies of both men were recovered."* As the files also reveal, Police Constable Terry had a growing reputation in the field of dowsing, and his skills were used on several occasions in matters of a similar, secret nature.

Britain's ***Daily Telegraph*** of July 20th, 1994 reported the following obituary: "Colonel Kenneth Merrylees, the water-diviner who has died aged 97, worked during the Second World War as a bomb-disposal expert, when he used his dowsing skills to find bombs with delayed-action fuses which had penetrated deep into the ground."

Today Big Business Use Dowsers

Hoffman-La Roche, one of the largest global pharmaceutical companies in the world, has used dowsing to locate water for its new chemical plants. La Roche needs large quantities of good water to process the chemicals into drugs. A company magazine quoted Dr. Peter Treadwell as saying, "Roche uses methods that are profitable, whether they are scientifically explainable or not." Well said Dr Treadwell skeptics take note.

The petroleum industry has used dowsing to locate oil wells. Paul Clement Brown, a MIT graduate and electrical engineer, used dowsing to successfully dowse oil wells for **Standard Oil, Signal Oil, Getty Oil, Mobil Oil,** and others. These companies would not waste time and money in employing dowsers if they did not perform consistently in locating new oil deposits deep underground now would they?

Medical Applications

Homeopaths and nutritionists use Dowsing and this intuitive approach often gives patients answers they would not obtain with a more linear method as it comes up with remedies about problems a practitioner may not even know how to address. Kinesiologists who muscle test may use dowsing with a debilitated client to locate the source of sickness or to find what is ailing the patient.

Mr Chris Johnson is a director and trustee of the British Society of Dowsers and chairman of the organisation's Health and Healing interest group. Based in the Midlands England, he is a professional dowser and tutor, and runs a relaxation and natural therapy business, EMPATHEIA, with his wife. Chris is also a spiritual healer and Reiki master and teacher. Chris uses dowsing to find food intolerance which stems from stress inside our body.
(See:http://www.foodsmatter.com/natural_medicine_comp_therapies/dowsing/articles/dowsing_all_johnson.html)

International Association of Health Dowsers (IAHD)

The IAHD is an association formed especially for qualified therapists, energy and health workers who use dowsing or would like to use dowsing skills to support their work.

It is also an association for those wishing to learn how to use dowsing and energy techniques to help their own health and the heath of others.

AIMS

- To act as a network and hub for therapists, energy and health workers using dowsing for health purposes.
- To disseminate knowledge of health dowsing as an aid to treatments and therapies to therapists, energy and health workers as well as members of the public.
- To share knowledge and news pertaining to dowsing and health via the media, association bulletins or newsletters and by holding annual conferences and networking events.

Mr Olof Jonsson: (October 18, 1918, Malmo, Sweden-May 11, 1998, Las Vegas) was a well-known clairvoyant whose abilities were similar to the extraordinary powers attributed to advanced yogis (*sidhis*, in Sanskrit). As a young man, he was tested extensively in Europe. When he immigrated to the US in 1953, J. B. Rhine, Director of the Parapsychology Laboratory at Duke University, conducted many experiments with him. Olof Jonsson was also involved in other high profile ESP tests, including one with Astronaut Edgar Mitchell on the Apollo 14 mission to the moon.

He also was chosen to be the psychic on the team which recovered approximately two billion dollars of gold buried in the Philippines by the Japanese during World War II. Two books were written about Olof, the first published in Sweden, and ***The Psychic Feats of Olof Jonsson***, by Brad Steiger in 1971. (ISBN 0137320167)

U.S. Air Force & the CIA

An extensive paper titled ***Paraphysics R&D Warsaw Pact*** report dated 30th of March 1978, written by staff at the Foreign Technology Division (FTD) at Wright-Patterson Air Force Base, Dayton, Ohio stated on page twenty-three of the document showed positive results from both the U.S. and Soviet Union research in the field of **dowsing**. Notably, a copy of the entire FTD document was sent to the CIA's Office of Science and Technology (OSI) shortly after its findings were published.

Adolf Hitler Used Dowsers During WWII

During World War Two U.S. Air Force's files reveal that even Adolf Hitler consulted German dowsers as a means to try and locate places where he could get a deep, restful sleep in between waging war on the Allies. The German Navy were convinced that the British were using dowsers to help locate German submarines, not knowing at the time that the code breakers at Bletchley Park in England had broken the German enigma code. The German Navy set up their own Pendulum Institute to help understand pendulum dowsing techniques and how to use this skill to help locate Allied shipping.

To Find Water, Gold, and Mineral Deposits

Mr J.P. Taylor (known as Peter Taylor) is professional gold consultant dowser with over 30 years experience and is based in North Wales, England. He has successfully found three separate gold deposits at the Clogau Gold Mine in North Wales, and found numerous Spanish Armada ships along the North East Coast of Scotland. He also found the Eugene Pergeline built in France in 1900. This ship sank off the Southern Irish coast on the 15th of March 1917. Mr J.P. Taylor found this ship 15 miles away from where the original sinking was reported by the authorities.

(See: http://www.prospectinggold.co.uk/index.html).

Here is Peter Taylor (left) taken February 2017 in Dubai verifying the existence of a new fresh water source for a water bottling company. Peter told me that this location was found by using his pendulum map dowsing technique. Peter will be returning to Dubai in March the same year to carry out a similar site survey and water drilling operation for the same client in another area of the country.

100% SUCCESS!
In the picture shown on the left we can see that Peter's dowsing skills taken in Dubai in February 2017 were 100% correct when the drilling machine hit a vast new drinking water source.

To Find Gold, Diamonds and Mineral Deposits

It is interesting to note that Mr J.P.Taylor has produced a table on his website showing the locations of new diamond deposits, and gold deposits for mining companies and of course ship wrecks. Peter Taylor like me believes that companies can save time and money in employing a trained dowsing consultant to accurately locate new mineral wealth or lost shipwrecks. In Mr Taylor's words:

"I have located 132 locations of potential gold fields and mineralized deposits around the world, such as 44 diamond fields and 10 platinum deposits." (January 2016).

Mr Louis Matacia Earned a Bachelor of Science in Technology in Land Surveying serving as a topographical surveyor in the U.S. Army, U.S Marines, Philippines and with licenses in six Eastern states. He taught dowsing techniques to U.S. Marines to locate networks of tunnels, traps, and wires. Mr Matacia has located oil reserves, buried treasure, water & irrigation wells, ground water, caves, tunnels, utilities, septic systems missing or lost objects or persons, and archaeological digs.

Dowsers Throughout History Past and Present

- Leicester Gataker
- Messr Jacques Aymar Vernay
- Uri Geller
- A. Frank Glahn
- Otto Edler von Graeve
- Henry Gross
- Larry R. Marshall
- Nils-Axel Mörner
- Karl Spiesberger
- Ludwig Straniak
- Solco Walle Tromp
- Hellmut Wolff
- Leonardo De Vinci
- Robert Boyle (father of modern chemistry)
- General Rommel of the German Army
- John Living
- Albert Einstein
- Hanna Kroeger
- Charles Richet (Nobel Prize Winner)
- Louis Matacia
- Olof Jonsson
- J.P.Taylor
- Jim Longton
- David Villanueva

A number of dowsing books and websites list the following people as either dowsers or believers in dowsing: Sir Isaac Newton, Thomas Edison. Dr. Karl Berg, Arch-Bishop of Salzburg, Henry the VIII, Vernon Cameron and General Patton. Reference to these learned persons will persuade readers that dowsing has aided humanity throughout history and continues to benefit us now in the 21st century, and beyond.

Maybe the greatest scientist that the world has ever known Albert Einstein performed impressive experiments throughout his life with a variety of dowsing devices. He later stated:

"The intellect has little to do on the road to discovery. There comes a leap in consciousness, call it intuition or what you will, the solution comes to you and you don't know how or why." "The truly valuable thing is the intuition, Imagination is more important than knowledge."

Good Research Is Vital To Successful Practical Treasure Recovery

There are so many expeditions that are arranged in a hasty fashion, where the treasure hunter has not bothered to carry out sufficient research or even thought about consulting a well trained dowser to help them locate whatever they seek! Why do these people waste thousands or even millions of dollars searching in the wrong place?

We see these people on TV programs trying to mine gold dust or nuggets in the USA, Canada, and other places of the world where they hope they will be able to just break even on their "investment" and maybe just maybe find more alluvial gold to make a reasonable profit before the treasure hunting season ends with the onset of winter or in the case of South East Asia when the wet season begins. Some of these people are so desperate and in debt they travel to Africa from the USA on a promise of striking it rich in a country like the Congo where kidnapping and murder of foreign visitors and gold miners is rife.

What a waste of time and effort. Why go through the uncertainty of not knowing whether you will be a successful gold prospector, when a good dowser would have told you where the gold bearing seam was located beforehand.

I strongly suggest that these people talk to Mr Peter Taylor beforehand as he has already identified ten new gold deposits in Canada that also includes two new Platinum deposits and eight new diamond deposits. In the USA alone he has located nineteen new gold deposits, and in the United Kingdom a further twenty six new gold deposits. Why try and reinvent the wheel when the donkey work has already been done by a highly experienced dowser that has over 30 years of dowsing experience!

It seems that poor research and planning will result in poor performance every time. This is also the case when it comes to searching the sea bed for lost treasure ships. Again marine salvage companies would rather spend thousands of dollars a day surveying the ocean floor with a narrow beam sonar fish for days on end wasting valuable time and human resources.

Why? Sailing back and forward, "mowing the lawn' in a zig-zag pattern searching for a target is both time consuming and very costly to the financier of the underwater search expedition.

Half the time maritime researchers are relying on old reports of where the ship was last seen from naval authorities that are outdated and are frankly not too accurate. Shipwrecks have a tendency to move far away from their last known position due to strong tides and underwater currents and are covered by thick layers of mud and sand! A side-scan sonar will not locate a wreck buried under 40 feet of sand!

Many of the Commercial Diving Organisations would argue that there are other ways that shipwrecks can be detected under deep mud and sand. These techniques include:

Sub-Bottom Profiling: A system employed to identify and characterize layers of sediment or rock under the seafloor. These systems also can be helpful in locating hard objects buried *beneath* the seafloor, such as shipwrecks. In sub-bottom profiling, a sound source directs a pulse toward the seafloor. Parts of this sound pulse reflect off of the seafloor, while other parts penetrate the seafloor. The portions of the sound pulse that penetrate the seafloor are both *reflected* and *refracted* as they pass into different layers of sediment. These signals return toward the surface, where they are detected by hydrophones towed by a surface vessel.

Multi-beam SONAR: Employs a multitude of individual SONAR beams to provide fan-shaped coverage of the seafloor, this system is similar to side-scan SONAR but with different data output. Side-scan SONAR systems continuously records the *strength* of the return echo or ping. Whereas multi-beam systems measure and record the time for the acoustic signal to travel from the transducer to the seafloor and back again to the ships receiver. Knowing the time, the distance to the seafloor can be calculated, and using the transmission angle from the transducer, the depth at each beam can be determined. Placing beam points (as many as 512 for some multibeam echo sounders) in a line produces data from which a contour for each ping can be developed; placing these contours side by side allows a three-dimensional representation of the seafloor to be developed.

Multibeam SONAR offers considerable advantages over conventional systems, including increased detail of the seafloor (100 percent coverage), confidence that all features and hazards are mapped without voids, the ability to map inaccessible areas (e.g., under jetties, structures, and vessels near breakwaters, in shoal areas, and adjacent to retaining walls), fewer survey lines (which shortens survey time), optimum seafloor detail for route and dredge programs, and the ability to comply with the highest order International Hydrographic Organization (IHO) and US Army Corps of Engineers (USACE) hydrographic standards.

Magnetometers: A valuable tool for underwater surveys, detecting the magnetic field anomalies that result when induced magnetic fields are superimposed on the earth's magnetic field, such as the magnetic anomalies created by ferrous material in the earth's magnetic field.

Magnetometers provide accurate and reliable data, since these devices do not directly measure the physical properties of the areas or objects of interest, the output signals of these sensors require some signal processing for translation into usable data.

Magnetometers are frequently utilized during pipeline surveys, shipwreck surveys, and when buried ferrous materials need to be located. Burial depth can be found by performing statistical analysis on shapes generated from magnetic field anomalies to gauge the size and shape of the metal target. A single magnetometer or with a multi-magnetometer device mounted on an ROV, mini submarine or used by a diver will aid in the search and discovery of lost ship wrecks, cannon and metal locations around the sunken vessel.

The chance of discovering a new shipwreck using conventional means is frankly limited by financial constraints, search time, inaccurate location data, inaccurate side scan sonar results, underwater currents, mechanical breakdowns, lack of equipment, underwater visibility and of course bad weather around the search grid area. A good dowser has none of these restrictions when carrying out a dowsed search for a lost shipwreck.

He or she will ask a series of direct questions that will result in where the shipwreck is located, the depth of water, whether the wreck is buried in the sand or mud, and also how far the debris field stretches from the main part of the wreck itself. The dowser CAN verify and identify the name of the ship and the number of cannon she had on board if necessary! The more questions the dowser asks the more answers come back to him or her, and a picture of how the ship came to rest at the bottom of the ocean and its precise location is achieved by the dowser.

If I was financing such a ship wreck search I would employ several good dowsers and pay them the suitable dowsing fees and expenses each and ask them to dowse the mapped search area in question and ask if they can locate where the shipwreck is located BEFORE I even get onboard a dive support vessel like the one for sale below:

For Dive Support Vessels
See: http://commercial.apolloduck.com/

For Submarines and ROV's talk to Alan Whitfield CEO of Silvercrest Submarines Ltd.

See: http://www.silvercrestsubmarines.co.uk/

3. <u>Your</u> Plan Of Action For A Successful Treasure Recovery

1) **Research**
   Study the geographical area you are interested in and collect all of the historical information you can, and all of the old maps and photographs. Compare old maps with new maps to see whether others may have been before you, and just maybe you may spy something of value others may have missed.

2) **Employ Dowsers**
   Ask more than one dowser to dowse your maps for treasure or lost artefacts. I suggest that you should employ three to four good dowsers that do not know each other. Then compare their findings. If more than 60% of their findings match and are positive, then verify with further research or a visit to the site armed with metal detectors, side scan sonar and ground penetrating radar.

3) **Plans For Recovery**
   If your new treasure site is found to be positive, (meaning that a target has been identified by a dowser and the verified using the appropriate electronic equipment to verify the existence of the item) then plan how you will fund the recovery operation, and list all of the equipment you will need to achieve your goal. Always have a recovery Plan A, Plan B and a Plan C to fall back on if one of your plans fail to come to fruition for any reason.

4) **Emergency Funds and Additional Costs to Consider**
   Always have a reserve fund put by for accidents, equipment failure, inclement weather, sickness, fatalities, and preventative maintenance scheduling on heavy excavation vehicles, generators, water pumps and the like. If the weather does turn nasty, do you have additional food and fuel reserves to see the bad weather period out or will you have to stop and abandon the project altogether. The key here is the dig when the weather is favorable to do so, and know when dry season starts and ends. Plan your work schedule accordingly to avoid snow fall, torrential rain, thick fog, permafrost, and very cold and very hot periods of the year.

5) **Making Good**
   If you have to dig a hole some 250 feet deep and do not find what you are looking for, then you must have the funds and the manpower to fill in the hole and make good around your treasure site. You cannot leave a big hole in the ground and think that no one will notice. You have a duty of care to humanity and to the wild animals that could fall into the hole. So make good and leave the site in a better way than you found it. Again this cost is yours and not the landowners!

6) **Site Safety And Security**
   What planning have you made to keep the site secure against looters?

   How will you secure any of the items that you find? Will you have a private security team to guard your treasure? If so will this team be armed and ready to tackle anyone who tries to steal treasure from you? Security and safety planning is very important and must be accounted for when you are planning your treasure adventure. Funds must be made available to ensure your safety and the safety of your recovery team.

7) **Permission**
   Have the necessary permission to search and recover **BEFOREHAND**. Please be aware of the treasure recovery laws in the country in which your target is buried or lost at sea and make sure that you have the necessary permits and landowner agreements in place before you even start to dig a hole! Failure to do this could see you arrested and fined for trespass, and any items that you have found will be confiscated from you. So please prepare all of the necessary documents before you start any recoveries. Please remember night hawks and treasure robbers are caught and go to jail and are fined heavily for digging up historical artefacts without permission.

Follow these seven pointers and you will become a successful treasure hunter who may decide to become a successful dowser too!

In the subsequent pages I have supplied you the reader with the history of the lost treasure together with the GPS locations of where I believe the treasure is located.

I have supplied the GPS latitude and longitude in degrees and minutes and in many cases the depth and type of treasure deposit.

If the reader wants to have a decimal location, then please go to Google Earth website and left click you mouse button onto the **Tools** button located at the top left side of the page. Then left click onto **GPS,** and then click onto Import to see Garmin or Magellan set up waypoints.

Note: The next few chapters have been taken from my first book in order to help you the treasure hunter find treasure successfully, these chapters are relevant in his book and have been used successfully by treasure hunters currently looking for buried Imperial Japanese loot in the Philippines.

4. Finding Buried Treasure

I have supplied three ways to help you locate quickly and identify whether your site is a veritable "gold mine" or just a place where others may have buried rubbish long ago.

This search technique assumes that you have lots of funds at your disposal that you could use to find potential gold burials. These techniques are:

A) Resistivity Ground Testing
B) Ground-Penetrating Radar Scanning
C) Spot Bore Drilling

A) Resistivity Ground Testing

The first resistivity ground test will prove two important things; for instance, whether a mass of metal exists underground that is worth further investigation. (Gold as a metal is very conductive, and will be found quite easily using this method of detection.)

This test will also highlight whether the mass of metal is stored inside a man-made tunnel or a natural cave system where the entrances have been blocked in the distant past.

Please note that this type of instrument will not tell you the precise depth of the object, only its location on your site.

According to Bob Fitzgerald, his Mother Load Locator ™ has found many gold bars in the Philippines, Greece, and the USA. This device will operate to a depth of 130 feet.

B) Ground-Penetrating Radar Scanning

Ground-Penetrating radar scanning proves to you that the cave or tunnels exist underground, and that the original soil strata have been disturbed by previous digging operations by persons unknown. The scan will also show any unique objects buried below the ground either in or outside a void, and give you an indication of the actual depth of the target in question. Many GPR systems will only show voids and disturbances under the ground to a depth of three to five feet, therefore another device needs to be used in order to detect objects buried at deeper depths.

This type of device cannot tell you whether the target is indeed gold, silver or indeed made from concrete, but only where the object is situated under the ground and at what depth.
The type of GPR scanning system you choose and whether the soil is highly mineralized will have an effect on results.

Two types of GPR are available: the first model uses a high frequency transducer, which means that the transmitted frequency will give less ground penetration and depth than the second model that uses a low frequency transducer, which will give more ground penetration but at a lower display resolution.

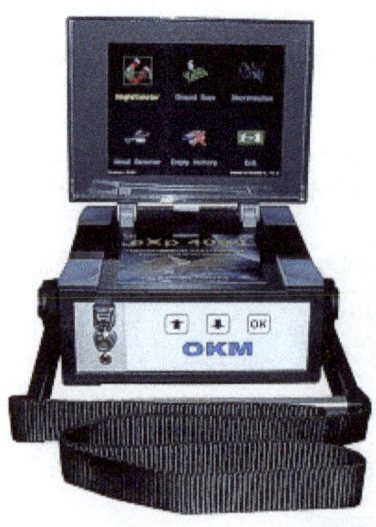

The OKM EXP4000™: Depth 25 metres; can detect voids and discriminate between different types of metal.

Note: Advances in metal detection are developing all of the time, and I therefore strongly suggest you investigate these new technologies before you spend thousands of dollars on the wrong type of search equipment. So do your research thoroughly. Please see Appendix for listing of deep search metal detectors.

All Trade Marks acknowledged.

C) Spot Bore Drilling

Once you have identified that "yes" you have a target and you know its location and its depth, then the decision has to be made whether you are going to hand dig down to the target or whether you are going to save time and hire or buy in a drilling rig for the job.

Portable water drilling rigs are used primarily for drilling water wells or for mining exploration.

These portable drilling rigs are usually transported to site on a trailer, and can be set for drilling within two hours. These rigs can be hired from the mining or water drilling companies, which usually charge by the metre drilled; the deeper the hole, the larger the cost. This one way you can verify that a target is located deep underground before committing to the added expense of hiring expensive backhoes and diggers.

See: http://www.drill2water.com/Water.html

All Trade Marks acknowledged.

5. Does Buried Gold Give Off An Aura?

The answer to this question is yes, gold and other metals give of an ionic plume that can be seen by some either early in the morning or at dusk. As dowers we pick up this energy once we are tuned into the frequency of the metal.

One man in particular used his psychic ability to actually see the aura floating above the buried and sunken gold on land and at sea. His name was **Olof Jonsson**, a gifted psychic who was born in Sweden in 1918.

He helped President F. Marcos locate the Japanese Battle Cruiser **Nachi** in Manila Bay by seeing the "purple plume" hovering over the wreck on a calm day. When the divers went down to investigate, they found to their surprise Olof had indeed put them right on top of the wreck's location.

This idea of buried gold giving off an aura or a plume, similar to smoke from an open fire, is not new. The ancient Incas in Mexico found gold by "seeing" the aura plume described, usually in the early morning when there was no wind and the weather was calm.

Not all of us have these gifts of seeing or feeling the presence of gold, however a very successful British treasure hunter has come to your aid and has mastered the art of photographing gold, silver, copper and other metal auras buried in the ground. This has taken him three years to perfect the process and to recognize the different colours that represent various types of metals buried under the earth.

Now using modern digital cameras with infrared filters fitted to the lens, the camera can capture these auras, and by using Photoshop software, the treasure hunter can verify where precious metal is buried prior to any excavations taking place. Steel, iron, copper, gold, silver, can also be identified using this technique to verify treasure deposits before you start expensive excavations. Identifying steel or cast iron objects beforehand is useful, for example if you think old bombs or other hazards may be around a buried gold cache.

David Villanueva has written an exciting book on this very subject, called *The Successful Treasure Hunter's Secret Manual: Discovering Treasure Auras in the Digital Age.*

(ISBN 978-0-9550325-5-4). Please see link: www.truetreasurebooks.com

In September 2012, David reported to me that one of his followers used the techniques described in his book and found thirteen gold coins weighing 110 grams at a depth of 1.85 metres. The infrared photo showed a massive aura on the surface of the sand. This technique works! I therefore suggest you invest in this fascinating book and use it to find your own hidden gold. Treasure hunting discussion links to photographing treasure auras:

See link:
http://treasurehunters.yuku.com/topic/494/ARE-TREASURE-AURAS-FOR-REAL?page=2#.TztxYMXUN_c

To watch a practical demonstration of David Villanueva with his digital camera photographing a gold aura and recovering four buried gold sovereigns using his metal detector:
See:http://www.truetreasurebooks.net/products-page/e-book/the-successful-treasure-hunters-secret-manual-discovering-treasure-auras-in-the-digital-age

Infrared Images Of Buried Gold From Known Treasure Sites

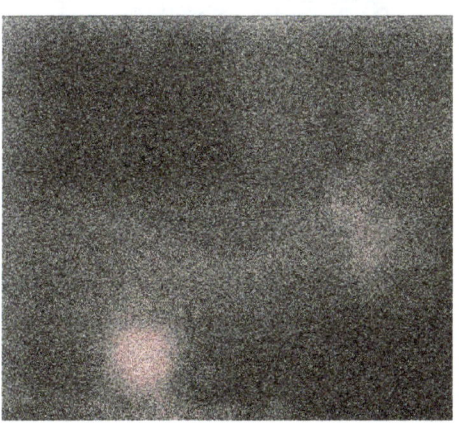

This picture (left) was taken of an area of ground where an old Japanese map and my dowsing told the owner of the land where the gold was located.

The owner decided to check the area out using his digital camera and an infrared filter, just as David describes in his excellent book *Treasure Auras in the Digital Age*. We can see clearly two gold deposits; the darker one will have more mass than the smaller aura on the right of the photo. The owner is planning to excavate this site when the weather is more favourable to treasure hunt. This technique can also be used to photograph a gold aura that will appear over a sunken ship wreck that carried gold bullion. The best images will be taken on a calm day between sun rise and at dusk.

In this picture we can see the infrared aura coming from an object buried in the ground. By using experimental infrared photography, using three different filters of varying light spectrums, you photograph known metal objects above the ground you can successfully identify which infrared light colour spectrum matches gold, silver, diamond, copper and iron..

You can build up a library of these colours on a database, which will enable you to easily identify these "matched" infrared colours of known metal objects above ground with infrared auras giving off metal objects buried below the ground as you photograph areas of interest with your digital camera.

Image A: Nazi Gold Bar   Image B: The Negative Image

Image A is a "known" Nazi gold bar, and image B the negative image.

We now can identify an inky dark blue colour matches gold, both above ground and below ground.

This technique can be used to verify a gold aura when an infrared image is converted into a negative image.
See image C below:

Image C: A Bluish Gold Aura: 100% confirmation that gold is buried here.

This process of taking a series of infrared digital photos of an area means that you can survey a lot of ground quickly and efficiently. Infrared photographs can be taken in rapid succession, transferred into a laptop and viewed on site within minutes, and areas with buried metal will be identified instantly, saving many hours in searching rough terrain with a metal detector. The other advantage is that these photographs can be taken early in the morning, or at dusk, when the surrounding temperature is not unbearable in hot climates. Remember: the longer the metal object has been in the ground, the better the infrared aura.

In the case of gold, this aura will be at its best when the sun has warmed up the ground all day, and the sun's rays have penetrated the ground during the day. The gold will retain this heat and will increase the infrared aura around the object at dusk and early in the morning when there is little wind and when air humidity is low. In Chapter 9 you will see an example of an infra red image showing a gold aura taken by Mr David Villanueva when he verified my dowsed findings close to Waltham Abbey, England.

Another Way To Detect Buried Gold

There are long range detection devices that can detect the ionic field that gold objects give off when buried in the ground for a long time. These devices are made by several manufactures would be one way to detect treasure hoards that have been buried over many years. One German manufacturer OKM may now have the solution to locate these gold items. This method of detection is called Ionic Detection Method (Ions Chamber System). The company has combined both the Ions Chamber System together with a Bionic Detection Method (Bio-Energy-System) where the OKM Bionic X4 long range gold detector is able to locate almost all gold objects independently of age including gold items not buried in the ground.

This type of detecting device is ideal to quickly locate areas where the treasure hunter is not sure in which direction the gold artifact is located. This type of device will not however give you the depth and precise location of where the gold artefacts are buried. You will still have to rely on a metal detector to give you the exact location and depth of your buried gold deposit.

See: http://www.okmmetaldetectors.com/products/longrange/bionic-x4.php?lang=en

Now that I have explained how to go about planning and searching for the lost treasures, I give you the treasure locations around the world in the following chapters, together with the GPS co ordinates and other valuable information to help you with your own treasure hunt. All you have to do is verify my findings with other dowsers or visit the sites mentioned with the appropriate detection devices mentioned in the appendix of this book. Now go and find your own treasure and piece of long lost history.

6. Nazi Treasure Lake Toplitz Austria

In the next three chapters I give you the reader the locations of buried treasure situated in Austria. The first place I want to mention in this chapter is of course Lake Toplitz. This lake is situated in a dense mountain forest high up in the Austrian Alps, ninety eight kilometres from Salzburg in western Austria. It is surrounded by cliffs and forests in the Salzkammergut Lake District within the Totes Gebirge region of Austria.

The lake water contains no oxygen below a depth of 20 metres. Fish can survive only in the top half down to 18 m, as the water below 20 metres is too salty, and an ideal place to hide SS Nazi treasure.

At this time, Austrian nature experts are demanding a ban on diving adventures in Toplitz Lake scuba divers still visit the area every year searching the muddy bottom for Nazi treasure."Every year we see at least 10 divers who come here hoping to locate the Nazi fortune although it is strictly forbidden," stated Mr Bernhard Schragl, the spokesman for Bundesforste AG, the body in charge of the area. Nature experts and forestry authorities are currently calling for the Austrian government to appoint a ban on all future diving activities and admit concern that the countless divers are threatening the ecological balance of the lake.

Several diving explorers have unfortunately drowned over the years after becoming entangled in the branches on the bottom of the lake however that hasn't stopped diver interest in exploring this area of Austria.

Time Line

On February the 23rd, 1945: Hitler's Reich was decimated and the Allies were destroying the Nazi regime. Meanwhile in Berlin, the Nazis were scrambling to move their most valuable secrets out of the city. A Jewish man, Mr Adolf Burger was expecting to die at the Sachsenhausen concentration camp situated 22 miles north of Berlin, simply because he knew too much about the Nazi plot to print fake currency which Hitler hoped would help bring down Britain and the United States during the Second World War.

"That meant I was privy to German state secrets, and knew that I would be murdered by the SS once my work was completed" said Burger.

When the project was ended, Burger was told to pack the counterfeit currency into boxes. These were then transported to the Nazis' Alpine Fortress situated in Austria.

The Alpine Fortress (*Alpenfestung*) was the World War II national redoubt planned by Heinrich Himmler in November/December 1943 for Germany's government and armed forces to retreat to an area from "southern Bavaria across western Austria to northern Italy. The plan was never fully endorsed by Hitler and no serious attempt was made to put the plan into operation.

By April 1945, time had run out for the remaining high command of the Third Reich. Hitler was dead in Berlin, and the Allies were closing in all around. Many of the last leaders of the Nazi regime fled into the Austrian mountains to make a last stand against the Allies. Others were to try to save some small part of the Reich in the hope of starting over one day, and Adolf Berger's work was essential to that plan.

No one would have ever seen the boxes again if it weren't for a 21-year-old Austrian farm girl called Miss Ida Weisenbacher. She saw where the secret cargo went and lived in the same house near Lake Toplitz where Nazi soldiers found her 71 years ago.

"It was five o'clock in the morning, she recalled, "we were still in bed when we heard the knock on the door, get up immediately and hitch up the horse drawn wagon, we need you.'" Demanded an SS officer.

The S.S. needed the wagon because the truck had reached the end of the road. Only horses and a wagon could make the journey across muddy tracks to Lake Toplitz. "An SS commander was there, who ordered us to bring heavy boxes as fast as possible to Lake Toplitz," added Ida Weisenbacher. She said each box was labeled with bold-painted letters and had a corresponding number.

She drove three wagonloads to the lakeside. "When I brought the last load, I saw how they went on to the lake by boat and dropped the boxes into the water. The S.S. guard on shore kept shoving me away but I saw the boxes were dropped over the side of the boat into the lake," stated Ida.

Earlier Searches

In July of 1959, German technicians working with ultrasonic depth finders and underwater television cameras pinpointed 16 cases in Lake Toplitz in Austria at a depth of between 38 and 44 fathoms. Several of these were brought up and found to contain perfect forgeries of British sterling notes to the value of £8,500,000 pounds.

The notes had been produced at the concentration camp at Sachsenhausen, near Berlin, and were part of a plan devised by Hitler codenamed *Operation Bernhard* to destroy the British economy.

The Search for Nazi Gold Using a Remotely Operated Vehicle

The Phantom is a deep-diving robot operated by Oceaneering Technologies from Maryland, USA and connected by a tether cable to a ROV pilot controlling the submersible on the surface. Mr Jeff Kowalishen was one of the pilots of the underwater craft: "It's hard to hide something from this type of equipment." He stated.

Oceaneering was the company that recovered the wreckage of the Space Shuttle Challenger, TWA Flight 800 off the bottom of the Atlantic Ocean and located the downed aircraft of John F. Kennedy Jr.

60 Minutes II hired Oceaneering to search every inch of Lake Toplitz and recover the boxes if they could be found. "No one has tried at Toplitz to do this, but we have done this type of work all over the world," said Mr Kowalishen.

In the winter of 1999 negotiations were started with the Austrian government and the country's forestry service. After being assured the project wouldn't hurt the environment, the Austrians agreed to lease the lake for 30 days, a very tight schedule for what the Oceaneering team was about to attempt, the search and recovery of boxes of gold bars on the bottom of the lake.

This particular expedition was to be the first comprehensive search of Lake Toplitz. The diving expedition would cost over $600,000, with major funding provided by the World Jewish Congress.

(See: http://www.worldjewishcongress.org/en/about)

The ROV Phantom propelled itself along near the bottom of the lake searching for lost Nazi treasure.

For 12 hours a day, the crew strained for some familiar box shape. But there was no hint of anything like Adolf Burger's boxes. It was possible the boxes were buried or covered in muddy silt long ago It was also possible, after 55 years, they had just crumbled away.

In nearly three weeks of searching, the submarine would cover more than 35 miles altogether. The 30-day deadline imposed by the Austrians was getting closer. And Oceaneering couldn't get a break from the lake. To the tethered mini-ROV, the lake floor was a minefield. Oceaneering expected trees but not underwater forests. The trees had fallen from the mountain over a very long period of time, and were stacked 60 feet high on the muddy bottom of the lake in some places. The Phantom would spend many days lost in this sunken forest deep below the surface. The team also had to contend with bad weather such as hailstorms and lightning.

A bolt of lightning struck the navigation system, and the search pattern the crew was following wasn't reliable anymore. But Mr Kowalishen wanted to carry on searching the depths of the lake, guiding The Phantom by dead reckoning. Then a small discovery was made, old pieces of wood that may have come from the Nazi boxes.

On the 28th of March 2014, the British Daily Express newspaper printed an article entitled:**" Has secret Nazi treasure been hidden in this beautiful lake for 70 years?"**

In this article, the nephew of a senior Nazi SS officer Ernst Kattenbrunner has now come forward and decided to tell the world what he knows about a hidden hoard of Nazi treasure buried in Lake Toplitz during the closing months of the Second World War.

Mr Michael Kattenbrunne stated in the newspaper article: "I can guarantee there is a lot of gold and vast treasures inside" Mr Kattenbrunne 79, has never spoken before about what he knew, but was encouraged to talk to an Austrian investigative reporter after she had produced a true story program about the Monuments Men, the U.S. Military led team that were ordered to find looted SS Nazi treasure in the closing months of the WWII.

Reports of a convoy of SS vehicles taking large chests to the lake in early May 1945 began to emerge soon after Germany surrendered, but no one saw the SS soldiers dumping boxes of gold into the lake at this time. I suggest that the most valuable riches were to be stored elsewhere **near** to Lake Toplitz.

Mr Kaltenbrunne also stated that he thinks these treasures are located where the counterfeit money and printing plates were found at the bottom of the lake over seventy two years ago.

A German WWII medal was found by chance in 2001 by a Dutch tourist diver in a second lake in the region. Lake Altausee that once belonged to Ernst Kaltenbrunner (left) was believed to have been dropped by the SS boss into the water as he moved through the area trying to evade capture. (See chapter 8).

Dowsing of the area resulted in me finding two gold targets, one in the lake and the second south of the lake buried in a tunnel system on the side of the mountain. This I believe is the location of another massive Nazi treasure horde. The local population will be able to confirm that where this treasure is located was in fact the old entrance to an old salt mine.

It is interesting that Mr Michael Kattenbrunne stated in the newspaper article: "I can guarantee there is a lot of gold and vast treasures inside".

Why would he state that the treasure is "inside" when in fact he should have stated that the Nazi treasure was underwater or at the bottom of the lake, and the word "inside", suggests that Kattenbrunne possibly knew that the main treasure hoard was *inside* a tunnel and **not** at the bottom of the lake as other historians have previously suggested.

The nephew substantiated further claims made by Austrian journalist Konrad Kramar in his book 'Mission Michelangelo' that Ernst Kaltenbrunner allowed Austrian miners in charge of the area to remove some of the paintings, prior to bombs being planted to blow them up whether this happened or whether the bombs were used as booby traps no one knows.

Does this mean that works of art where destroyed or did Kaltenbrunner order the closure of the salt mine with explosives. I would assume the latter was true.

Another important assumption would suggest that the main SS Nazi treasure delivered by trucks was **not** dumped into the lake, but instead stored inside a salt mine tunnel close by to the lake, and when the tunnel was full of the SS Nazi hoard the troops blew the entrance shut with an explosive charge.

I decided to dowse for the lost Nazi treasure on the 27th of February 2011. The picture on the next page shows my dowsed findings. One gold deposit in the lake and a massive gold, gems and lost artwork deposit inside an old salt mining tunnel system in the forested area south of the lake.

On the 30th of September 2016, I dowsed the area again to verify that the gold targets were still there. I can confirm that both gold targets are still in the GPS locations are shown on the following page.

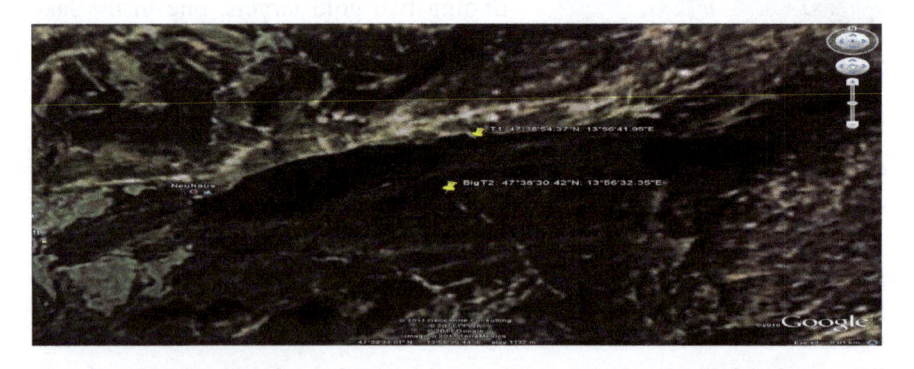

Latitude N	Longitude E
T1: (8 boxes gold bars): 47°38'54.37"	13°56'41.95" 194 feet deep
Big T2: (gold, art and jewels): 47°38'30.42"	13°56'32.35" 158 feet down in tunnel complex

In December 2015 whilst I was visiting friends in Thailand I was told a story that two divers both brothers from Austria had been employed by the Austrian Government to secretly search and salvage any Nazi gold bullion from the Austrian Lake. These two brothers over the past 10 years have been very successful in this regard, and would holiday in Pattaya a sea side resort every year when the summer diving operations in Austria came to an end.

If this story is true, then the Austrian Government would have probably cleaned out most of the SS Nazi treasure from the numerous lakes that held gold bullion long before anyone was allowed to dive with ROV's into the depths to try and find lost Nazi treasure.

If this is so, then the only Nazi treasures worth finding now are the ones buried on the side of the mountain overlooking Lake Toplitz. My findings still show that there are boxes of gold bars still at the bottom of Lake Topitz at a depth of 194 feet dowsed in 2016 buried in the muddy bottom 3 feet down

Dangers of the Lake Today

Lake Toplitz was used by the German Nazis scientists as a secret military laboratory for experimental weapons testing between 1943 and 1944. Lake Toplitz shores were secluded from major settlements so the Germans chose this lake for secret experiments. Any explosions carried out during WWII would not be heard by anyone. Scientists dropped torpedoes, bombs and other weapons to check their effectiveness against Naval Allies at sea.

The German Kriegsmarine or German Navy sponsored these experiments. Many of the explosives are still resting on the lake bottom. The local Austrian populations often call Lake Toplitz Devil's Warehouse or Demon's Hole as a reference to a possible 4 tons of unexploded ordinance on bottom of the lake waiting to go bang, so please be aware of this fact before you go diving for gold in Lake Toplitz!

7. Lake Lünersee Nazi Treasure Locations Austria

At the bottom of Lake Lünersee another Nazi lost treasure worth $50 million is waiting for a treasure hunter to find near Strasburg in the heart of the Austrian Alps. The treasure was made up of jewels and gold confiscated by victims of the Dachau Concentration Camp, that housed 30,000 prisoners in 1945, the same year in which a group of Nazis ran away with the treasure before being captured by Allied Forces.

Dachau was not only a prison for Jewish people, but for about 1,173 Nazi war criminals imprisoned there. One of them, a former officer of the SS condemned to death, told Dr. Wilhem Groß the existence of an impressive treasure. Dr. Groß, an Austrian born physician, identified the place described by the prisoner and shared this information with Mr Edward Greger, a U.S. Army intelligence officer stationed in Austria in 1952.

Dr. Groß and Greger followed the same route as told to the doctor by the German officer towards the Lake Lünersee on the Austrian border with Switzerland. According to the German officer, the commandant of the camp loaded the treasure into 4 boxes and with the help of his assistants before leaving Dachau, transported the hoard to Lake Lünersee. The informer was one of those officers conspiring to escape with the treasure and all those involved went their separate ways until the time to recover the treasure hoard would arrive after the war was over.

As the years went by the area that was familiar to the SS Officers in 1945 changed dramatically and geographic features such as trees, and the erosion of the shore line of the lake made finding the exact location of the buried treasure very hard to find indeed. These changes could be seen in 1952.

Four years later, Dr.Groß and Greger returned to the lake after calculating where the treasure was buried, but a damn constructed in 1956 increased the lake's level submerging the boxes under nearly 75 feet of water. Greger returned again in 1990, this time when the lake recovered its original level after the damn was emptied for some days, but the treasure was not found possibly sunk deeper somewhere inside the lake due to weight of the boxes.

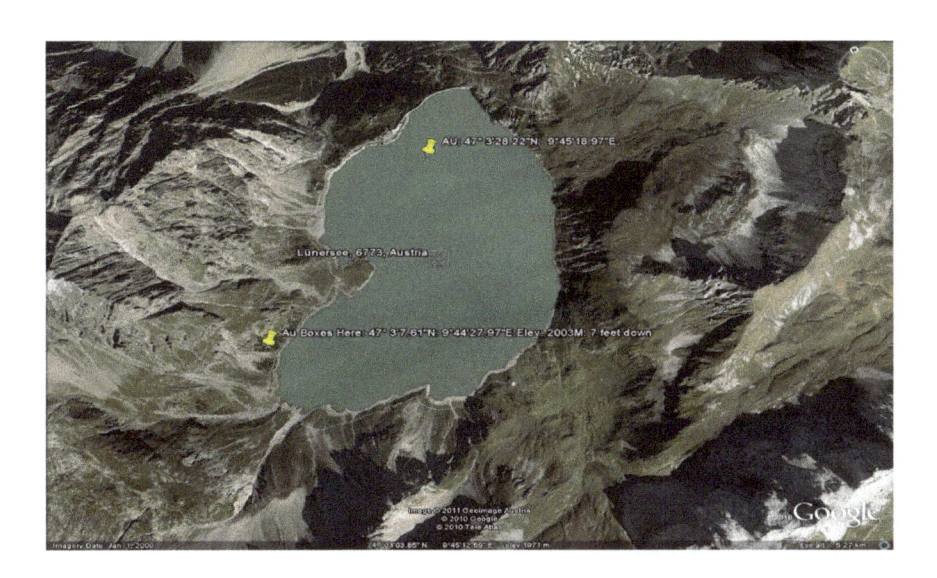

Dowsed by the Author on: 2nd February 2011

Latitude N	Longitude E
Gold Bars in 6 Boxes : 47°03'28.22"	09°45'18.97" 95 feet deep in mud
Gold/Jewels in 4 Boxes: 47°03'61.00"	09°44'27.97" 7 feet deep under big rock

8. More SS Nazi War Treasure Alt Aussee Region of Austria

The third Nazi buried treasure locations are to be found around the Alt Aussee region have been known for many years to be the site to search for Nazi war treasure, and certainly the most dangerous. Legends of hidden wealth are commonplace, and are backed up with a great deal of historical documentation. The Allies removed ninety truckloads of the most priceless arts and treasures from the underground salt mine to safety here in 1945. It is said that they did **not** find it all. The recovered treasure was valued at over $300,000,000 and consisted mostly of rare paintings, sculpture and other valuable artworks stolen and confiscated during World War II. The complex Nuremburg testimony disclosed that most of the Alt Aussee treasure was in the salt mine complex, and the rest **spread over** the countryside.

Dowsed Locations of Treasure from WWII: South of Bad Aussee:

Target 1: Latitude: 47°35'49.57" N   Longitude: 13°46'56.99"E
Target 2: Latitude: 47°35'39.69" N   Longitude: 13°46'20.37"E

North East of Bad Aussee and South of Grundisee:

Target 3: Latitude: 47°36'34.63"N   Longitude: 13°51'05.11"E
Target 4: Latitude: 47°36'13.23"N   Longitude: 13°51'51.67"E

36

William Canaris, the Nazi intelligence chief until he fell during the 1944 General's Plot against Hitler, is supposed to have buried a hoard of treasure in the Aussee. Supposedly, it is stored in one of the mountain caves there, and contains Persian rugs, tapestries and a huge store of narcotics worth millions of dollars.

On Christmas day, 1944, Gestapo chief Ernst Kaltenbrunner arrived at Alt Aussee and rented a house called Villa Kerry.

Ernst Kaltenbrunner aged 43
(04 Oct 1903 - 16 Oct 1946)

Near this location he buried a large number of treasure caches, including 100 pounds of gold coins, hundreds of thousands of American dollars, several chests of diamonds and other gems and a large collection of rare and priceless stamps. Buried in the gardens of the **Villa Kerry** which he rented, American troops found almost $3,000,000 in loot and no one knows how much more remains.

Another historical source states: Ernst's personal treasure trove was 50 kilograms of gold bars, 50 cases of other gold, $2 million USD, $2 million in Swiss francs, five cases of jewels, and a stamp collection worth 5,000,000 gold marks.

Ernst Kaltenbrunner Arrest

It was in a hut about twenty miles just over a mountain range from Lake Toplitz and Alt Ausee that Ernst Kaltenbrunner was eventually found and arrested by US soldiers. He was executed in 1946 after being trialed at Nuremberg, the highest ranking Nazi SS officer to appear at the trial.

Villa Kerry dowsed by the Author on 01 January 2017: **No Gold** aura was found in this location. Villa Kerry is next to Loserhütte and is located in Styria, Austria.

Villa Kerry Latitude: **47°38'44.52"N** Longitude: **13°45'53.64"E.** As you can see on the previous page treasure deposits are buried not too far from Villa Kerry.

9. Waltham Abbey Treasure England

The dissolution of the monasteries was one of the key features of the reign of Henry VIII. The monasteries were seen as being a cornerstone of Papal authority in England and Wales. After various pieces of legislation were introduced into England that ended the Pope's authority during the early 1530's, the monasteries became the focal point of the king's vicious attack as it was assumed that they would remain loyal to the Pope and not the King of England.

Resistance to Henry VIII

Pilgrimage of Grace banner bearing the Holy Wounds of Jesus Christ

There were many reasons that the population living in northern England rose up against the King. A poor harvest of 1535 had led to higher food prices, and many rebelled against the way Henry VIII had discarded his wife Catherine of Aragon and executed her in 1536 for so called adultery and treason. The local churches and abbeys were the centre of community life for thousands of people and a resistance group was formed on 13th October 1536 called The Pilgrimage of Grace and lasted 1 year and involved some 40,000 participants until it was crushed by Thomas Cromwell and his soldiers. Once order was restored, Henry showed no mercy.

The head of each religious house thought to be involved were declared a traitor in an act of attainder and executed. Therefore, after their execution all this 'private' property transferred to the Crown as was required by an act of attainder. Any monks or residents from these houses were forced out onto the streets.

However, even after the Pilgrimage of Grace had ended, many powerful and rich monasteries remained, and those that had an income of more than £200 and therefore did not come under the 1536 Act and were south of the area affected by the Pilgrimage of Grace.

Action against these houses was taken, and Cromwell sent out commissioners to each of the houses. Those that seemed prepared to fight were noted but Cromwell had told the commissioners to leave these houses once they had spread some degree of fear in them.

The method used by the commissioners to persuade each head of a religious house was to make a threat you pay up 'if you love the king'. With the example of what had happened to abbots in the north for their 'disloyal' behaviour to the king during the Pilgrimage, many abbots succumbed to royal pressure. In 1539 an act was passed in Parliament that stated that any religious house that had surrendered its property voluntarily to the Crown was part of a legal act, as would be any future surrender of property. The act also included a statement that there could be no challenges to the validity of the king's title of ownership once a monastery had voluntarily dissolved. If the king then transferred ownership of titles, these too could not be contested in a court room.

The British government's commissioners went about their task with great energy. There is little doubt that the threat posed by the government led to many heads of religious houses handing over their land and wealth just as Henry and Cromwell would have wished. However, there were some abbots and religious house leaders who would not be bullied. They had to face the full force of the law, as it was perceived then. The Abbot of Glastonbury led what was a very wealthy monastery, one of the wealthiest in England.

He was executed and the buildings in the monastery were all but destroyed. The land passed to the king. **The Abbot himself was charged with secretly hoarding gold and "other parcels of plate, which the Abbot had hid secretly from all such commissioners".** I have dowsed the area that surrounds the Abbey and my findings will remain secret. By 1540, over 800 monasteries had been dissolved. The process had taken just four years.

Harold Godwinson (later King Harold II) rebuilt the Abbey in 1060 and was buried there after his death at the Battle of Hastings in 1066.

In 1120 the church was rebuilt in Norman style and in 1177 Henry II re-founded the church as an Augustinian abbey. At this time, extensive building works were carried out, traces of which can be seen in the Abbey grounds today.

The Augustinian abbey was a popular place for kings to stay during hunting trips in nearby Waltham Forest. Henry VIII was a regular visitor and on several occasions was accompanied by Anne Boleyn.

The Legend of the Holy Cross of Waltham

The story of the foundation and early history of Waltham is told in the manuscript 'De Inventions Sanctce Crucis Nostras' written by one of the canons in the twelfth century.

In the year 1035, a miraculous black marble crucifix or holy rood was discovered by a peasant, after a vision, at Montacute in Somerset, South West England.

The wealthy landowner, named Tovi the Proud, who was standard bearer to King Cnut, decided that the cross must be placed in one of the great religious foundations of the country. It was placed carefully on a cart pulled by 12 white and 12 red oxen, but when Tovi commanded that the cart should set off the oxen refused to move. As each religious house was mentioned to the dumb animals Winchester, Westminster, Reading, and so forth but the oxen still would not move a muscle.

Tovi the Proud finally remembered the little settlement of Waltham in Essex, where he had a hunting lodge as he was Lord of the Manor, and where there was a tiny Saxon church not much more than a hut. When Tovi mentioned Waltham the oxen set off and walked without direction from Somerset to Waltham.

Tovi built a new church for its reception at Waltham. He appointed two priests to the church and gave rich endowments for their maintenance. His devout second wife, Gytha or Glitha, (the daughter of Osgod Clapa), presented a splendid golden and jewelled crown, bands of gold and precious stones to adorn the figure. And the cross became the object of pilgrimage.

On his death, his son succeeded to some of his possessions but lost others, including Waltham, which King Edward the Confessor granted to Harold Godwinsson, Earl of East Anglia, the son of Earl Godwin of Wessex, and future King Harold II, the last Anglo Saxon King of England. At this point in history the whereabouts of the black marble cross and all of the bands of gold and jewels are a mystery. We can only assume that all of these items were kept by either the two priests appointed to safe guard these religious treasures and later by the Abbot of Waltham Abbey. As the Dissolution came nearer to Waltham Abbey, the Abbot had to make a decision. Do I hand over all of these religious treasures to the Kings men or do I find a safe hiding place for them? He was to make a decision to flee with the riches of Waltham Abbey north towards a safer haven as we will see.

Greedy King Henry VIII

The immediate effect of the Dissolution was to transfer vast tracts of land to the Crown. Monastic land was worth at least three times as much as existing royal landholdings and Henry also acquired vast amounts of gold and silver plate, worth as much as one million pounds, but he wanted more money and wealth to pay for wars with France and Scotland.

The seizure of monastic land gave the Crown the possibility of complete financial independence. If Henry VIII had exploited this new found wealth wisely and prudently, he and his successors might never have needed to call on Parliament again for funds.

The sad fact was that between the years 1543 and 1547, Henry had to sell most of the land he stole from the monasteries to pay for expensive wars with both France and Scotland. It is fact that Henry had changed the British landscape forever, and leaving hundreds of great monasteries and Abbeys in ruins for what gain?

One of the last Abbeys that King Henry VIII ordered destroyed and looted was his favourite. This was Waltham Abbey situated outside London in Essex. The King loved to spend long weekends here hunting in the nearby woods and dining very well on the game that he and his courtiers hunted locally. It was said that the Abbot had been tipped off long before Henry's soldiers arrived to ransack all of the wealth of the Abbey. The Abbot had time enough to organise a large flat bed cart pulled by 6 large oxen. This cart was hastily filled with all of the gold and silver plate and many religious crosses and the wealth of other Abbey's in the area.

The Abbott gave instructions to the monks to head north away from the Abbey and to hide the treasure in nearby woodlands. Alas the heavy cart had to pass through a water meadow north of the Abbey, and the wooden wheels became struck in the boggy water logged soil. The poor monks had only one option to dig a pit and to hide some of the treasure inside.

They managed to travel another 150 metres, and again the cartwheels became struck in the mud. This time the monks dumped the remaining treasure into the irrigation ditches close by and covered the items with cut marsh reeds. They then managed to move the cart clear of the area, and then opened the river sluice gates allowing the River Lee to completely flood the water meadow covering the hidden treasure locations.

When the soldiers arrived from London they found a small amount of the treasure. According to the account of the Monastic Treasure Confiscated by Sir John Williams written in 1836, the soldiers collected 479 oz of gold plate, 251 oz of parcel gilt plate, and 439 oz of white metal. A small fraction of the treasure stored at the Abbey. We can conclude that the Abbot escaped with the cart and oxen packed with treasure to a friendlier place to the north of the Abbey, possibly situated around St. Albans Abbey and the Abbot's lodgings at the time.

I dowsed the water meadow situated north of Waltham Abbey on the 27th of February 2011 and found several gold and silver auras just off the old track that is still visible even today. This track is situated on the right side of the old water meadow. In the time of the Dissolution of the monasteries all of this land belonged to Waltham Abbey. Today is it owned by Lee Valley Regional Park Authority.

I mention this important site simply because my dowsed findings were verified by David Villanueva who visited the site shortly after, my dowsing activity and photographed the area in question using his Canon digital camera with infra red filters where I said these religious items were buried by the monks in 1540. He confirmed to me that he had in fact photographed a gold aura coming off the ground where I said the treasure was buried at a depth of eight feet.

David Villanueva then contacted the landowner who stated that no permission would be given for treasure hunting on the ancient water meadow area. They did however suggest that if a formal archaeological plan was provided then they may be willing to provide a license for excavation.

If there is a professional archaeologist, or archaeological group, out there looking for an exciting project in Essex, then please contact the author of this book.

One of the gold auras photographed on Walham Abbey meadow site by David Villanueva

The GPS location will be kept secret until such time an excavation can be carried out with the written permission from Lee Valley Regional Park Authority. See Link: (http://www.leevalleypark.org.uk/).

10. Capt. Avery Treasure, Cornwall, England

History denotes that the treasure of pirate Capt Avery is buried in the high cliff near Beagles Point, South of Black Head, Cornwall, near the Lizard. Several attempts have been made to locate it without success....until now that is!

See: http://www.piratespades.org/pages/history/pirates/avery-john.html

Because of the positions of these targets permission will have to be granted by the landowner and the coast guard for you to be allowed to explore this site due the dangerous cliffs and rocky terrain. Do NOT attempt this site without written permission from the landowner HM Coastguard and the necessary safety training and rock climbing equipment. Further verification of my findings will have to be carried out before attempting a search and recovery operation. Contact: HM Coastguard, Pendennis Point Castle Drive, Falmouth Cornwall TR11 4WZ. Phone: +441326 310800 Or 01326 310800 if you live in England.

Latitude N	Longitude W
Treasure 1: 50°0'22.01"	5°6'48.95"
Treasure 2: 50°0'20.48"	5°6'51.03"
Capt. Avery Treasure: 50°0'19.97"	5°5'49.00" 12 feet down

11. The Merchant Royal Wreck Cornwall, England

On the 23rd of September 1641 late on a Thursday night The Merchant Royal was lost at sea ten leagues from Lands End, Cornwall, South West England. This ship was carrying gold and silver bullion worth millions of dollars in today's prices. To date no one has found this treasure laden ship until now.

This British merchant ship was rumoured to be the wreck found by the U.S. Company Odyssey Marine Exploration in 2007 and known only by the codename "The Black Swan".

But after lengthy legal battles, Odyssey was ordered to hand over coins recovered from the wreck to Spain, suggesting that the ship was really a Spanish frigate. And *not* the ill fated Merchant Royal, maybe Odyssey should have consulted a dowser beforehand, and I strongly suggest also in the future when they are looking for new ship wreck targets to carry out costly search and salvage operations.

At sea, a league measures three **nautical miles** (3.452 miles or 5.556 kilometres). The original story above states that the ship was lost ten leagues from Lands End. Please look at my October 2016 dowsed findings below:

Therefore 10 leagues are equal to 34.52 miles. When I measure from Lands End to the debris target the distance is 28.03 miles and the furthest point is 33.67 miles. In 375 years the wreck debris has decayed and drifted 14.5 miles in a North Easterly direction from the main gold location situated 34.52 miles off Lands End, Cornwall, England.

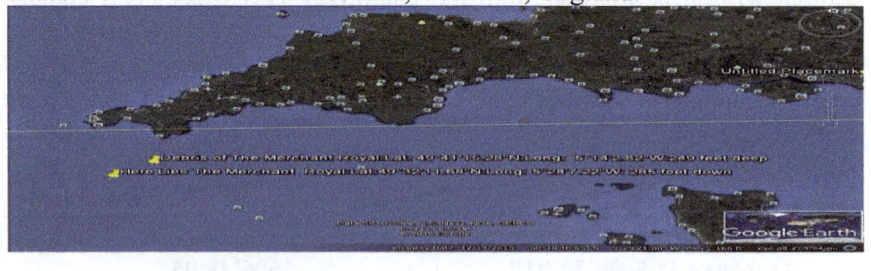

Latitude (North)	Longitude (West)
Debris Of The Wreck : 49°41'15.28"	5°14'02.82" (249 feet down)
Merchant Royal: 49°32'11.68"	5°14'02.82" (285 feet down)

12. King John's Lost Treasure The Wash England

King John of England (1167-1216)

King John also was known by another name, that of John Lackland, the rightful King of England between the years 1199 until 1216.

John Lackland was born on the 24th December 1167 and was the youngest son of Henry II. At the time John was not expected to become the heir to the throne of England.

Henry II died in 1189, and John's older brother was crowned King Richard I. While besieging the castle of Chalus in France whilst fighting against King Philip II, Henry was mortally wounded and died on the 6th of April 1199. King John was crowned King of England soon after his brother's death.

King John reputation with his people and the land barons that managed the land in old England was very bad indeed. Between the years 1202 and 1204 King John had lost all of the lands he once had captured in France to the French King Philip II. John was given the nickname "Soft Sword" and was humiliated both by the French and his British subjects.

Many scholars of history say that John was an evil lecherous man who loved to kill his captures in cold blood and chase after other noble's wives and daughters which resulted in several nobles rebelling against him.

With mounting debts from failed battles abroad, King John demanded more and more taxes and payments from his land Barons and ordinary people who were sick and tired of being broke. His continual extortion for more and more money, gold silver plate from the church led to many rebel

Barons declaring civil war against the King and his men. In 1215 civil war broke out between the King and his subjects.

In June 1215 a new charter was drafted by the Archbishop of Cantebury known as the Magna Carter which stated that the law is for everyone, and that the king was not above the law. The King was as much under the law of the treaty as his barons and subjects.

In addition, the charter disallowed the Sovereign King to trespass on the rights of the individual, and the rights of a free man could not be imprisoned, exiled, deprived of his property or destroyed just because the King wished it without due law and process.

King John signed the Magna Carta at Runnymede, Surrey, England under duress to end the rebellion with the barons, but was unhappy to do so The treaty took away his power to rule cruelly over his subjects and the peace process did not last long, in 1215 the First Baron's civil war begins.

King John's campaign against the rebel barons was successful in the beginning, but the rebels had decided to ask for help from the French. Prince Louis of France had claim to the throne of England, and landed his soldiers on the coast of Kent in May 1215. King John's shipping fleet was badly damaged by storms, which made the way clear for the French forces to invade British shores. Because of this uncertainty King John and his baggage train were travelling from place to place and it was on one of these journeys disaster struck.

How King John Lost His Treasure

The assumptions that historians had made in the past is that King John's baggage train travelled separately from the King, and was lost on the west side of the Wash where the Wellstream flowed out into the Wash, now known as the river Nene.

At the time the Wellstream was a marshy delta estuary made up of many streams that ran into the Wash and was affected by the ebb and flow of the tidal waters from the North Sea flowing into the Wash in 1215.

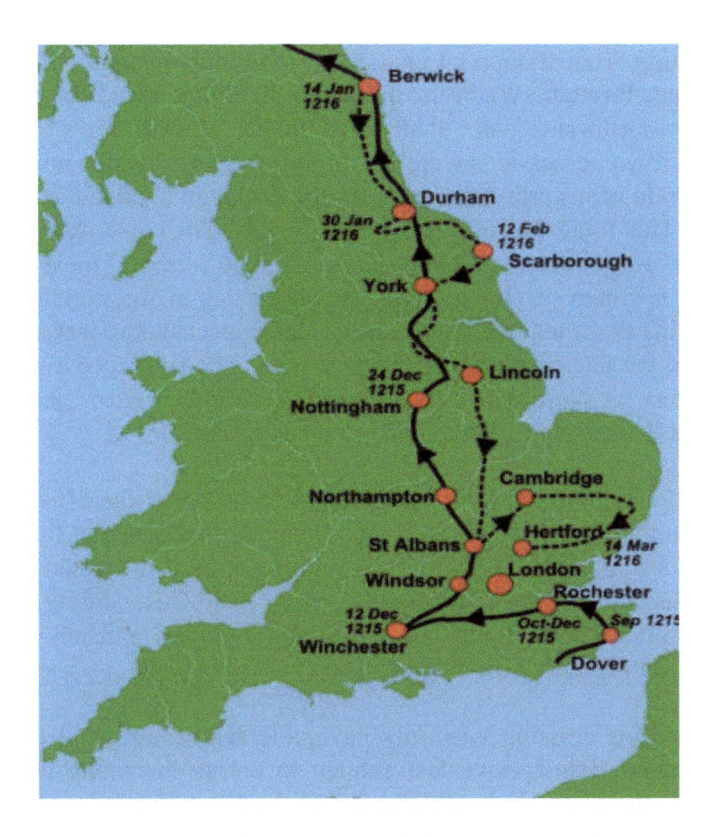

King John's military campaign from 1215-1216 (Wikimedia Commons)

Historical Timeline

In early October 1216, King John and his men arrived in the port town of Bishop's Lynn. (Now known as modern King's Lynn).

The baggage train attempted to across the mouth of the Wellstream on the 12th October 1216 travelling from Bishop's Lynn to Wisbech then on to Sleaford. Other historians say that the King was travelling from King's Lynn to Spalding. The number of wagons and men that made up the baggage train vary in size, some say that the main carts carrying the Royal Regalia numbered between three to seven wagons. The length of the baggage train was between a quarter to one and quarter miles long. If this was the case, it would make sense that a portion of the baggage train would have escaped the tidal flood water entirely, and the surviving solders raised the alarm.

On departing from Bishop's Lynn, King John had apparently chosen the safer route through Wisbech in Cambridgeshire avoiding the wash altogether. Historians state that King John's crown jewels and other valuable crown possessions were lost in **marshland** when the horse-drawn baggage train of his army attempted to cross without a guide the causeway and ford. This route was usable only at low tide. The horse-drawn wagons moved too slowly for the incoming tide or flood tide, and most were lost with only few men surviving. Some say on the day in question there was a "Stolen Tide that runs two hours earlier than expected, and it was this tide that sealed the fate of the Kings baggage train. The King died a week later of dysentery at Newark Castle on the 18th October 1216, and he was succeeded to the throne by his 9-year-old son, Henry III.

The location of the accident is supposed to be somewhere near Sutton Bridge, on the River Nene. The word: **"near"** this means that the treasure is located a short distance away from Sutton Bridge. The name of the river changed as a result of redirection of the Great Ouse during the 17th century, and Bishop's Lynn became King's Lynn as a result of Henry VIII's rearrangement of the English Church.

This dangerous crossing was only navigable at low tide, and the horse-drawn wagons didn't move fast enough to outrun the rising tidal water flow. The baggage train containing all of the Kings wealth sank into the soft estuary sandy mud as the waters flooded the doomed wagons, horses and men drowned trying to take a short cut that resulted in their doom.

There are three theories as to what happened to King John's treasure:

The baggage train was lost on the western side of the Wash and was lost near to Sutton Bridge.

The second theory suggested by Historians state that the baggage train travelled with King John and had become lost somewhere between Wisbech and Walsoken.

The third theory suggests that the baggage train was lost along the old causeway crossing between the villages of Tydd Gote (Tydd Go'ut) and Wapole St Peter or Wapole St.Andrews.

We will examine all of these theories and dowse all of the areas for the location of King John's lost baggage train, and reach various conclusions as to where the treasure lays buried under soft mud, and sand some 60 feet under the fields of the Lincolnshire countryside.

We have to make some assumptions, namely:

The Baggage Train would cross the Wash at the point where the distance would be minimal.

The crossing would have been done in secrecy to avoid unnecessary problems with the land barons and angry locals opposed to the King.

The baggage train had crossed the wash and was in trouble when it tried to cross the Wellstream between Sutton Bridge and Long Sutton.

So let us look at the historical facts and the searches that have been carried out to find King John's lost treasure.

The Hunt Goes On

During the early part of the 20th-century, several privately sponsored archeological attempts had been made to discover the exact location of King John's long-lost treasure, on 10-miles of reclaimed land between Sutton Bridge and Wisbech. Modern scientific equipment, such as the magnetic variometer method were implemented, from the headquarters of Fen Research Ltd., located at Dovecote Farm in Walpole St. Peter, which had been purposely formed to search for King John's treasure.

The research company was financially sponsored by the wealthy American called Mr James R.H. Boone of Baltimore, and included on the board Sir Francis Hill and Sir R.E. Mortimer Wheeler, keeper of the London Museum. Nothing was reported to be found.

In 1964 a British TV documentary called "Tonight" filmed a documentary explaining the location of King John's treasure. Two historians from Nottingham University explained where they thought Kings Johns treasure could be located in a field near to the old well- stream crossing. Professor James Holt explained that King John had crossed the Wash several times without incident in the past, one three days before the disaster, and his baggage train would travel between 30 to 40 miles per day.

The King should have completed his journey between Kings Lynn in the east to Spalding in the west within one day. This did not happen, instead King John stayed the night at Wisbech (possibly he was a sick man needing rest) suggesting that something terrible had happened to his baggage train north of his location. We must assume that some of men did survive and were able to report back to him about the disaster.

Professor Holt also stated that King John more likely than not had two sets of Royal regalia's with him, one that was made in 1215 and the second set that was made in March of 1216.

The first set may have been sold by the King to fund his civil war with the Barons of England, or could have been lost in the Wash along with his baggage train that some say consisted of seven wagons. Professor Holt also explains that the second Royal regalia survived the wash crossing disaster and was used in 1220 at the crowning of Henry III.

The Professor also says that he would surmise that the King would have carried a substantial amount of 13th Century silver pennies to pay for his soldiers and staff.

Below I have recreated the map that professor Holts shows on the 1964 Tonight documentary, to make a few conclusions of my own based on my and others dowsed findings.

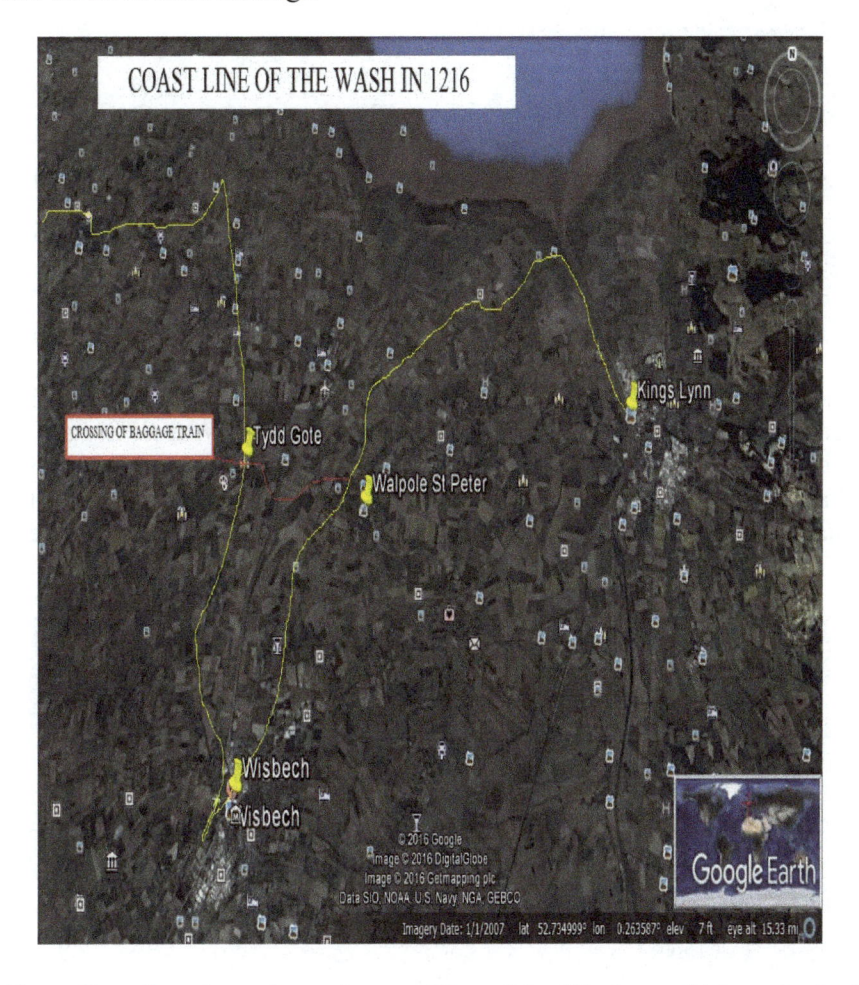

The yellow line shows how the coastline of the Wash would have looked like in 1216.

Professor Holt has assumed that there was a crossing point shown in red between Walpole St Peter and Tydd Gote. I have dowsed this route and found no evidence that the Kings treasure was lost between Walpole St Peter and Tydd Gote.

The Picture above shows the possible causeway that existed in 1216 between Tydd Gote (Tydd Go'ut: ***Tide Goes Out***) and Wapole St Peter or Wapole St.Andrews slightly to the North of Wapole St Peter As professor Holt states in the documentary, the baggage train had to cross not only the tidal estuary flowing back and forth into the wash but also the river Nene at Tydd Gote.

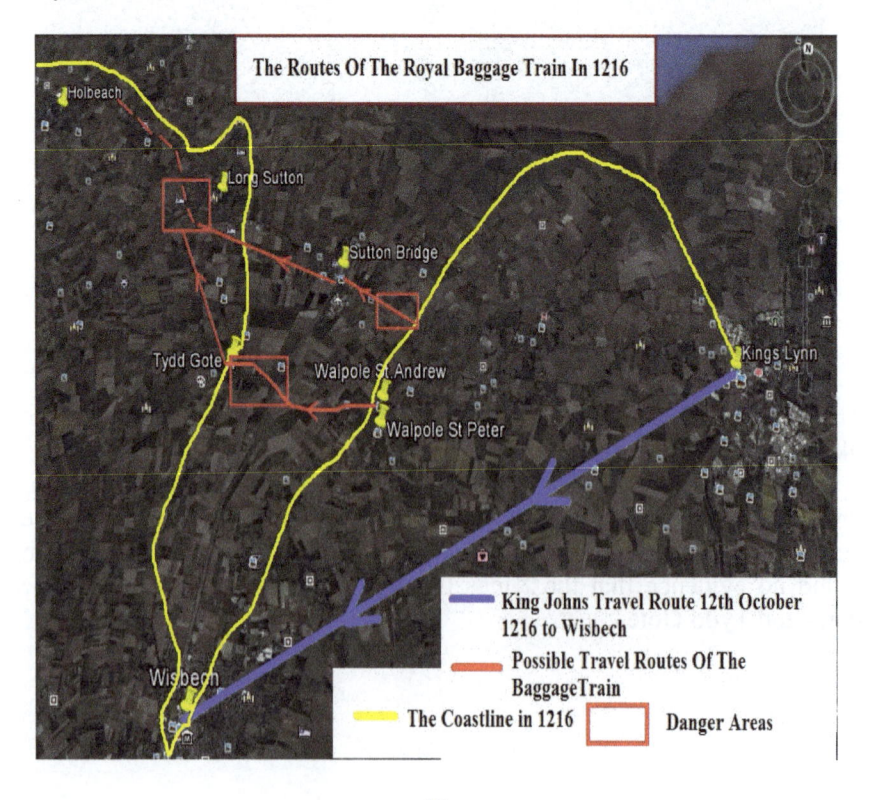

54

In the second part of this documentary a colleague of Professor Holt, a professor Evans was looking at the marine sediments of the wash and found by accident that he and his students *may have* found the remains of the part of the baggage train, when the drill bit used to collect sand core samples became damaged when it hit something very hard deep in the sand. He concluded that they had recovered samples of old 13th century iron nails and small amount of gold and silver which would have fallen into the layer of quicksand some 40 plus down in the estuary sediments in the 12-13th Century. Again, there was no evidence to suggest that he had found the Kings Baggage train.

In 2011, another documentary was uploaded onto You Tube that was made in 2003 by Andy Humpries film maker entitled: **King John, Search for the Treasure** Part 1, 2 and 3 in which two British treasure seekers named Walton Hornsby and his brother in law Philip Haydn-Slater called upon the services of Jim Longton a professional British dowser to find the location of King John's treasure. Jim "found" the location of part of the baggage train, and core samples produced small pieces of wood but no evidence of the Kings lost treasure.

Since reclamation began in the 16th century of the estuary between Long Sutton and Sutton Bridge, The Wash House (now the Bridge Hotel) marked the start of the safe track and it was possible to hire guides to help the travelers and also the drovers with their herds of cattle, flocks of sheep or geese safely over the marsh.

The year is 1216, King John I had lost his battles with France and was very despondent he had few friends now in England and had to find people that were loyal to the King in a land where the Land Barons had decided that the King's extortion of raising more taxes and ignoring feudal laws to pay for more wars with France meant that when the King and his men wanted to travel from town to town they had to do so in secret so that the land Barons would have little idea where the King would be at any one time.

The King had to be constantly on the move to avoid running battles with the Baron's army.

It was in this situation that I believe King John tried to cross the Wash and the Wellstream in secret that was his undoing. It is well known that the Kings baggage train had in the past crossed without incident, but this was due to the fact that the Kings soldiers would have paid for the services of a guide who would have known all about the times of the wash tides, and where to travel across the marshes safely, avoiding incoming tides and dangerous quick sands. I think that on the day of the disaster King John had a very good reason not to tell anyone that his baggage train was going to cross the wash from Kings Lynn on the way to his final destination at Spalding. His baggage train must have been carrying the Kings crown jewels that had been safely stored at Kings Lynn. The King had decided to have them moved inland away from the French Prince Louis who could have invaded the port of Kings Lynn at any time, and had to move the royal regalia to a safer location in this case the market town of Spalding was chosen by the King who still had loyal supporters living in the town.

The King had given orders to his generals that they must avoid the normal crossing area of the Wellstream, and to find another place to cross that was not well known to the regular traveler that used the wash regularly. He wanted security and secrecy, and he knew that if he was seen travelling with the baggage train this would bring about unwanted attention from the land Barons that would have had spies out on the main roads looking out for the King and his men.

The reason I state this now is that the remaining baggage train that was lost in quick sand and marsh in an area not frequented by the normal traveler in the year 1216!

The dowsed locations that I have and the dowsed locations of Jim Longton and others verifies that the baggage train was lost in an area that at the time was indeed marsh and probably could have been referred to as part of the Wellstream or river Nene and a collection of streams flowing into the wash. This area has until just recently been identified and verified using new Laser Satellite technology which shows the region in question to be water logged marsh and very boggy even in King John's time!

Historians have said that the carts carrying the oak trunks holding the kings crowns, jewels and other treasures was lost in the marshes and NOT in the Wash east of Sutton Bridge.

Below we can see that the only area that had marshes was on the western side of the wash way heading away from Sutton Bridge towards Long Sutton in the east along the Toll road that was once called the Washway, which is now is the A17 main road. Below picture 2 shows a lidar image clearly showing the marshy area South East of Long Sutton, part of the tidal Wellstream in 1216.

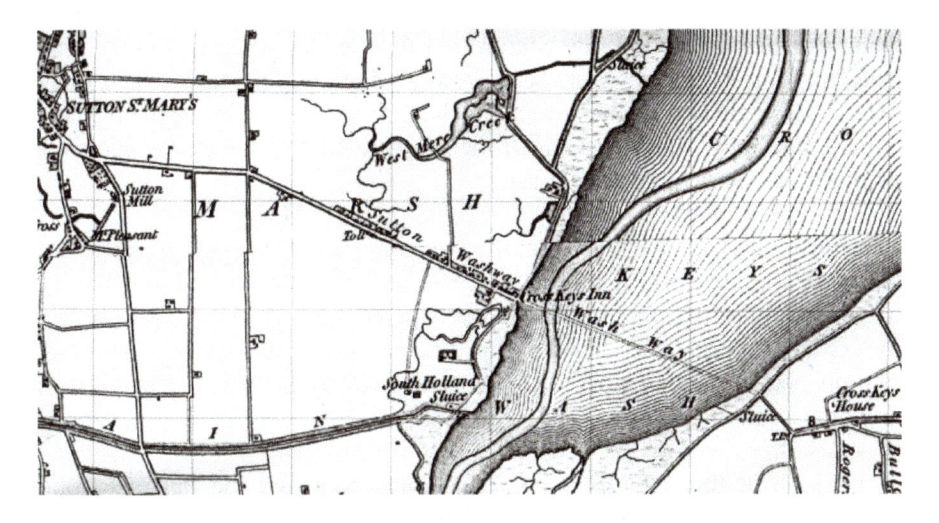

An Old OS Map of the 1800's

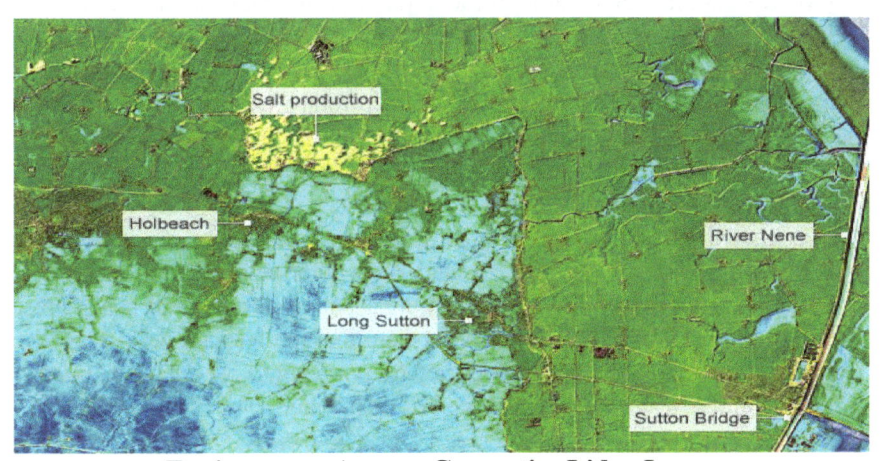

Environment Agency Geomatics Lidar Image

Lidar (**L**ight **D**etection **A**nd **R**anging) A lidar uses a laser to transmit a light pulse and a receiver with sensitive detectors to measure the backscattered or reflected light. Distance to the object is determined by recording the time between the transmitted and backscattered pulses and using the speed of light to calculate the distance travelled.

This area between Long Sutton and Holbeach is now farm land and would now mean that the baggage train may have crossed between Wapole in the east to Tydd Gote in the West. This crossing was successful without incident. It was when the baggage train took to the old country lanes heading north towards Long Sutton that disaster hit when a country road suddenly turned into a grassy bank byway which was passable when there was a slack tide from the Wash and help from a local guide who knew where the deadly running sands of the Wellstream were located as the river and streams drained into the Wash.

We must conclude therefore that the baggage train was trying to avoid the main road on the eastern side of the Wash at Sutton Bridge and to get away from unwanted attention that made the baggage train go across country and travel from Tydd Gote, north along deserted lanes on their way to Long Sutton and then pick up the main road towards Holbeach and onward towards Spalding.

Let's look at this journey now: The Kings men and the baggage train would have travelled from Tydd Gote possibly on the A1101 heading north towards Tydd St. Mary. They went through the village on the Church way road west until then came to the T junction with Cross Gate and Draw Dyke. The baggage train then headed north along the Cross Gate, until they reached the cross roads with Spendla's Lane and Roman Bank. The Roman Bank was an embankment that even today was higher than that of the marshy fields it rose some 7-15 feet high in places and was used by the travelers to cross the Wellstream.

The baggage train followed the Roman Bank north passed the T junction with Markillie Lane, up to where the Roman Bank intersects with Winters Lane. The Roman Bank road follows a half circular path to the left and heads north once more towards the A17. It was near here that the baggage train was lost. The men and horses were terrified as they tried in vain to get out of the marshy quicksand and a raising two meter swell of tidal water.

Many carts were scattered in a shambolic line but were lost without trace as night came and a heavy fog swallowed up the men, horses, wagons, carts, soldiers cattle, and the King's treasure. The treasure lays some 60 feet down in a layer of soft estuary mud and quick sand in a field where barley grows. I have dowsed the fields in this locality and have found that the baggage train went down in two separate fields some quarter of a mile apart from each other.

The sad fact was that the King's officer in charge thought he was home and dry. He and his men would have been if it was not for the stolen tide being two hours early on that terrible day in the year 1216.

The exact locations of the Baggage train will remain a secret until we have verified our findings and then we can reveal to the world what we have discovered.

Our recovery group will now use photographic infrared techniques mentioned previously to pinpoint gold auras emanating from the fields that we have identified as the possible site of the doomed baggage train. Once we have these images and they are identified as positive, we will then ask for permission from the farmer to use ground penetrating radar and deep search metal detectors to pin point the targets that are of interest.

Permission to excavate the area will take some time and considerations regarding animal and human remains will have to be factored into the recovery costs of any excavation and the filling in of any deep pits that are made by excavators and the restoration of the land to its former glory must also have to be funded and paid for after we have concluded our dig. Archaeologists would want to carry out a field survey and record where the horses, men and wagons lay in the ground, and precise position of the Kings wooden carts and wooden chests and relics. This site would be a treasure trove of historical finds trapped in sand and lost in time awaiting discovery.

13. Loch Arkaig Treasure Locations Scotland

The **Treasure of Loch Arkaig**, sometimes known as the **Jacobite Gold**, was a large amount of gold coins provided by the Spanish to finance the Jacobite rising in Scotland in 1745, and still rumoured to be hidden at Loch Arkaig in Lochaber, Scotland.

In 1745, Prince Charles Edward Stuart (or 'Bonnie Prince Charlie') arrived in Scotland from France and claimed the thrones of Scotland, England and Ireland, in the name of his father, James Stuart ('the Old Pretender'). Although Charles asserted that his venture was supported by Louis XV of France, and that the arrival of French forces in Scotland was imminent, France had little intention to intervene on the Stuarts' behalf. However, some limited financial support was supplied by both Spain and the Pope.

Spain pledged some 400,000 livres (or Louis d'Or) per month for the Jacobite cause. However, getting this money to the rebel army was very difficult. The first installment (sent via Charles' brother Henry who was resident in France) was dispatched in 1745. The French sloop *Hazard* (renamed *the Prince Charles*) successfully landed its monies on the west coast of Scotland. Unfortunately for the Jacobites, the riches were soon captured by Clan Mackay who showed loyalty to King George II.

In April 1746, the ships *Mars* and *Bellona* arrived in Scotland with 1,200,000 livres of gold coins (another Spanish installment, plus a large French supplement). However, on learning of the Jacobite defeat at the Battle of Culloden on the 16th of April, the ships left, unloading only the Spanish money at Loch nan Uamh, Arisaig on the 30th of April (the same place from where the Prince had disembarked the year before, and would later embark for France). Seven caskets of Spanish gold arrived in Scotland. By this time the Jacobite cause was lost, and with the army scattered the Prince and his lieutenants now in hiding, the money was to be used to assist the Jacobite clansmen (then being subjected to the brutalities of the government forces of the Duke of Cumberland) and to facilitate the escape of leading Jacobites to Farnce and the rest of the continent.

Six caskets (one having been stolen by McDonald of Barrisdale's men) were brought to Loch Arkaig (just north of Fort William) and hidden. Their secret location was entrusted to Murray of Broughton, one of the Jacobite fugitives. Murray began the distribution to clan chiefs, but when he was apprehended by the government (and later turned state's evidence) the treasure was entrusted first to Locheil, the chief of Clan Cameron, and then to Macpherson of Cluny, head of Clan Macpherson. Cluny was hiding in a cave at Ben Alder, which came to be known as 'the cage', and when Charles briefly joined him there, Cluny had control of the money, which was **still hidden** at Arkaig.

Bonnie Prince Charlie escaped Scotland onboard the French frigate *L'Heureux*, and arrived back in France in September 1746. The fate of the buried money is still not clear. Macpherson of Cluny is believed to have retained control of it, and during his long years as a fugitive was at the centre of various futile plots to finance another uprising. He remained in hiding in his Highland 'cage' for the next eight years.

Meanwhile, a cash-strapped Charlie was constantly looking for his money, and at least some of it came to him later, paying for the minting of a campaign medal in the 1750s. However, it is said that all of the gold was never recovered. Charlie, years later, accused Cluny of embezzlement. Whatever the case, the gold became a source of discord and grievance among the surviving Jacobite members.

The trail then goes cold. However, the Stuarts' papers (in the possession of Queen Elizabeth II) record a host of claims, counter-claims and accusations among the Highland Chiefs and Jacobites in exile, as to the fate of the monies. The historian Andrew Lang (who was one of the first people to research the papers since Walter Scott secured them for the Crown) recorded, in his book *Pickle the Spy* (1897).

The sordid tale tells of the involvement of both the Prince and his father in trying to locate the monies. The Stuart papers also include an account from around 1750, drawn up in Rome by Archibald Cameron that indicates that Cluny had not or could not account for all of it.

Latitude N	Longitude W
T: 56°57'1.43	5°4'43.50 3 feet barrel of gold coins
T1: 56°57'8.73	5°5'22.12 4 feet barrel of gold coins
T2: 56°57'2.82	5°4'42.77 3 feet barrel of gold coins
T3: 56°56'55.30	5°4'30.19 5 feet barrel of gold coins

According to Clan Cameron records, some French gold coins were found buried in nearby woods in the 1850s. The barrels of coins were not all buried in the same location this would have been done for obvious security considerations. Any recovered gold coins are considered to belong to the Crown, in this case the current Queen of England or the next in line to the throne of England (Prince Charles or his son Prince William Windsor).

14. The Treasure of Largo Law Scotland

Largo Law and the area surrounding it have many folk legends. The actual hill of Largo Law is volcanic in origin, and was said to have been created when the Devil dropped a huge boulder and part of the outcrop on the top of Largo Law is known as the Devil's chair, and has seven steps leading up to it.

There has always been tale of a gold mine or hidden treasure which lies under the hill. It is said that sheep grazing the area were often found with yellow tinged coats, a result of feeding near the site of the goldmine.

One tale about the hidden treasure talks about a ghostly guardian who needs to be approached to reveal the buried treasure.

There was a brave shepherd who lived in Balmain, which is on the Northwest slope of Largo Law. A ghost was said to haunt the vicinity, and to have in his possession a great secret to impart by anyone bold enough to approach him.

One night the shepherd took courage and approached the dark shade, asking what kept him from his rest. The phantom said that if he came to a part of the hill at eight o' clock he would learn where treasure was concealed. However there were two conditions which needed to be fulfilled.

"If Auchendowie cock doesn't crow, and the herd of Belmain his horn doesn't blow, I'll tell where the gold is in Largo Law".

The shepherd, being a thorough man promptly went a killed all the cockerels within hearing distance of the place. He also approached the local herder, a young man called Tommie Norrie. He told him not to blow his horn at the appointed time for any reason on pain of death.

The time of the meeting drew near, and the Shepherd went on to the slopes of Largo Law and approached the phantom, as the local churches rang eight, the phantom turned to the shepherd to impart his secrets. Just at that very moment a horn blast travelled down off the hills, Tommie Norrie had either forgotten the bargain or did not care to keep it. The phantom was silent for a moment then cried in drawn out tones:

'Woe to the man that blew that horn, for out of that spot he shall never be borne.'

At these words Tommie Norrie dropped dead on the spot as if struck by some unseen force. His body could not be moved from where he fell no matter how hard people tried, and so eventually a stone cairn was piled about his body.

Latitude: 56°13'56.94"North Longitude: 2°55'33.40"West

I dowsed the hill in September 2013 and found a small gold aura suggesting that this alluvial gold dust is coming from a crack or fissure in the rock itself. A place where sheep can easily go to find water but man would have to squeeze into the crevice in order to see where the alluvial deposit is located very close to a spring that rises out of the ground.

Treasure Trove Under Scots common law the Crown has ownership rights to treasure, in the specific sense of items wholly or partly composed of precious metal (gold and silver). This aspect of the law has given its name to the whole portable antiquities system.

See:
http://www.treasuretrovescotland.co.uk/About/TTU_and_SAFAP.html

See: http://www.treasuretrovescotland.co.uk/Documents/TT-code-Jan-2016.pdf.

15. The Royal Charter Ship Wreck, Anglesey Wales

Above: The Royal Charter broke up on these rocks near Moelfre.

The ***Royal Charter*** was a steam clipper which was wrecked on the east coast of Anglesey on 26th of October 1859. The precise number of dead is uncertain as the passenger list was lost in the wreck, but about 459 lives were lost, the highest death toll of any shipwreck on the Welsh coast. It was the most prominent victim of about 200 ships wrecked by the Royal Charter Storm.

This steam ship was used on the route from Liverpool to Australia, mainly as a passenger ship although there was room for some cargo. There was room for up to 600 passengers, with luxury accommodation in the first class. She was considered a very fast ship, able to make the passage to Australia in less than 60 days.

In late October 1859 the ***Royal Charter*** was returning to Liverpool from Melbourne. With a complement of about 371 passengers (with a crew of about 112 and some other company employees) included gold miners, some of whom had struck it rich in Australia and were carrying large sums of gold about their persons. A consignment of gold was also being carried as cargo. As she reached the north-western tip of Anglesey on 25th October Captain Thomas Taylor, was advised to put into Holyhead harbour for shelter. He made the fatal decision to try and make Liverpool however, Off Point Lynas the ***Royal Charter*** tried to pick up the Liverpool pilot, but the wind had now risen to force ten on the Beaufort scale and the rapidly rising sea made this impossible. During the night of 25th/26th October the wind rose to force 12 *'hurricane force'* in what became known as the 'Royal Charter gale'. As the wind rose its direction changed from E to NE and then NNE, driving the ship towards the east coast of Anglesey. At 11 p.m. she anchored, but at 1.30 a.m. on the 26th the port anchor chain snapped, followed by the starboard chain an hour later.

The crew cut the sails loose help reduce the drag of the wind, but the *Royal Charter* was driven inshore with the steam engines unable to make headway against the force of the gale. The ship initially grounded on a sandbank, but in the early morning of the 26th the rising tide drove her onto the rocks at a point just north of Moelfre on the eastern coast of Anglesey. Battered against the rocks by huge waves whipped up by winds of over 100 mph, she quickly broke up and sank under huge waves.

Left: ***The Royal Charter Memorial, Llanallgo Churchyard.***

Mr Joseph Rogers, a member of the crew, managed to make it ashore with a rope line, enabling a few people to be rescued, and a few other passengers were able to struggle to shore through the surf. Most of the passengers and crew, a total of over 450 people, died. Many of them were killed by being dashed against the rocks by the waves rather than drowned. Others were said to have met a watery grave, weighed down by the belts of gold they were wearing around their bodies. The survivors, 21 passengers and 18 crew members, were all men, with no women or children survived. A large quantity of gold was said to have been thrown up on the coasts near Moelfre, with some local families becoming rich overnight. The gold bullion being carried as cargo was insured for £322,000, but the total value of the gold on the ship must have been much higher as many of the passengers had considerable sums in gold, either on their bodies or deposited in the ship's strong room.

Many of the bodies were buried in the local churchyard. Exactly a century later in October 1959 another ship, the *Hindlea,* struck the rocks in almost the same spot in another terrible gale.

The aftermath of the disaster is described by Charles Dickens in *The Uncommercial Traveller*. Dickens visited the scene and talked to the rector of Llanallgo, the Rev. Stephen Roose Hughes, whose exertions in finding and identifying the bodies probably led to his own premature death soon afterwards. Dickens gives a vivid illustration of the force of the gale:

So tremendous had the force of the sea been when it broke the ship, that it had beaten one great ingot of gold, deep into a strong and heavy piece of her solid iron-work: in which also several loose sovereigns that the ingot had swept in before it, had been found, as firmly embedded as though the iron had been liquid when they were forced there.

The disaster had an effect on the development of the Meteorological Office as Captain Robert FitzRoy, who was in charge of the office at the time, brought in the first gale warning service to prevent similar tragedies.

In recent years the site of the wreck has been popular with scuba divers. Much of the gold which was not washed ashore was in fact recovered by salvage divers in the months after the wreck, but many artefacts have been recovered in recent years.

The veteran diver Sydney Wignall recalls discovering a large gold bar on the wreck site in the early days of scuba diving in his book *In search of Spanish Treasure: A Diver's Story.* The bar was jammed solid in some iron work on the sea bed, he used his knife to try and free the bar. He found the saw edge of his knife cut through it very easily, but before he could cut all the way through his air supply ran out and he had to leave it, the flakes of metal stuck on the saw blade of his knife were essayed and found to be almost pure gold.

Before he could return to recover it another storm hit the site and he was unable to relocate the gold bar. There is no record of this bar being recovered, so there is a very good chance it is still down there somewhere.

The remains of The Royal Charter wreck lie in very shallow water (8-22 feet), but the visibility at the site is usually very poor indeed. The wreck was smashed into pieces in the original storm and has broken up even more since.

Reports suggest that Australian gold sovereigns from the Royal Charter still occasionally turn up **on the beach after major storms**.

In 2011, it was estimated at least 79,000 ounces of gold were on the ship before the disaster, worth £77.6 million today. About 80 per cent of gold aboard the wreck has now been recovered, leaving millions of pounds' worth of gold remaining scattered on the sea bed even today.

It is said that the ship was battered by 60ft waves and 100mph winds. The ship snapped in two while less than 50 yards from the coast.

I dowsed this location in 2007 and found gold auras in two different parts of the Moelfre Peninsula. It would seem that some of the gold was buried possibly by a local on land after the disaster. I believe bodies were washed ashore or drifted on the tide along the shoreline where the gold carried in money belts came to rest on the sea bed after many storms since the sinking and now awaiting discovery.

I decided to re dowse this area on the 7th October 2016 to see if there was any gold still awaiting discovery. Please see the picture below:

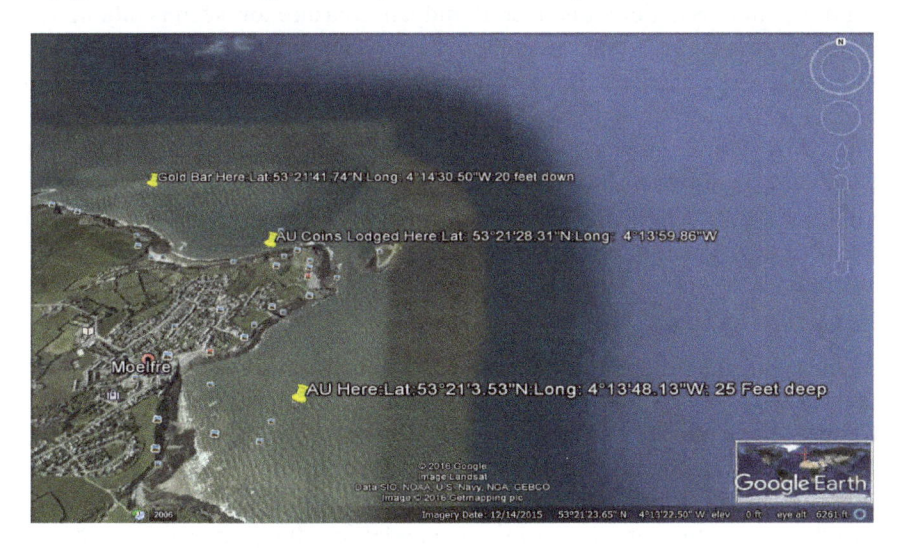

From my dowsed findings there are clearly gold coins and gold nuggets still to be found in the shallow waters off Moelfre.

16. Rennes-le-Château Treasure in France

Rennes-le-Château is a medieval castle village and a commune in the Aude département, in the Languedoc area in southern France, an area known for its towering mountains, deep gorges, forests, caves, wild remote plateaus and access to the Mediterranean.

Recent Reputation and Fame

The modern reputation of Rennes-le-Château rises from rumours dating from the mid-1950s and not from the lifetime of a local nineteenth century priest Bérenger Saunière, who was alleged to have mysteriously acquired and spent large sums of money (despite the existence of much evidence proving the contrary). Published by French Editions Belisane from the early 1980s onwards, the evidence ranged from the archives in the possession of Antoine Captier, which includes Saunière's correspondence and notebooks, and the minutes of the ecumenical Trial between Saunière and his bishop between 1910-1911 which are located in the Carcassonne Bishopric.

Today Rennes-le-Château has become the centre of conspiracy theories claiming that Saunière uncovered hidden treasure or secrets about the history of the Church that threatened the foundations of Catholicism. Since the mid-1950s, the area has become the focus of increasingly sensational claims involving the Knights Templar, the Priory of Sion, the Rex Deus, The Holy Grail, treasures of the Temple of Solomon, the Ark of the Covenant, geometric alignments, and the burial site of Jesus Christ. The village now attracts visitors who look for hidden treasures and evidence of a conspiracy, much to the displeasure of the locals.

Sceptical views

Almost all historians reject these conspiracies as nothing more than fantasy. Monsignor George Boyer in 1967 (Vicar General of the parish of Carcassonne), Rene Descadeillas, Jacques Rivière, Jean-Luc Chaumeil, Jean-Jacques Bedu, Vincianne Denis, Bill Putnam, John Edwin Wood, and Marie Francine Etchegoin state the stories of Saunière's 'mysteries' were based on nothing more than a minor scandal involving the sale of masses, which eventually led to the disgrace of both Saunière and his bishop. His 'wealth' was short-lived and he died relatively poor. Other aspects of the Rennes-le-Château legend derive from forgeries created on behalf of Pierre Plantard.

Dowsed by the Author: 22nd November 2010

The only presence of gold that I found here was at this location outside of Rennes-le-Château village. This deposit can be accessed via a small path that leads down from the village to an area of sandstone. It looks like there could be below the surface a small cave twenty feet down that was filled in long ago. The amount of treasure is small, suggesting a less than 20 gold coins stored inside a clay jar.

Latitude: 42°55'36.38"N Longitude: 2°15'45.79"E

17. Lost Nazi Treasure Locations in Deutschneudorf Germany

Deutschneudorf is a small municipality in the district Erzgebirgskreis, in Saxony, Germany and the region was primarily known as the location for buried Nazi gold. This site, an abandoned copper mine in the Ore mountains, was identified by radar scans as having a large amount of dense metal believed to be too dense to be copper, and therefore it was concluded that there may indeed be a vast amount of Nazi gold buried inside an abandoned copper mine very close to the village.

On February 26th 2008, treasure hunters in the small sleepy town of Deutschneudorf announced to the world that they were ninety per cent certain that they had found SS Nazi gold in a tunnel system ten metres down north east of the village, near to woodland once frequented by the Nazis during the Second World War.

The mayor of Deutschneudorf, Mr Heinz-Peter Haustein told the German website, Spiegel Online that he had found the location of tons of gold and possibly the whereabouts of the lost Amber Room taken by the Nazis from the Soviet Union in 1941.

From information received from Mr Christian Hanisch a drilling operation was launched based upon a war time document belonging to Christian's late father showing the co-ordinates of the closed vaulted tunnel recorded when he was a Luftwaffe air force signaler stationed close by during WWII.

Haustein has reportedly kicked Hanisch out of Deutschneudorf village [source: CNN]. The two treasure hunters argued about where to dig and whether to suspend the search until scientists and engineers arrived to assess the situation. Hanisch now says he does not believe the treasure hunters have found the Amber Room at all. He later stated "it's just plain old gold". Whether he meant the deposit was natural mineral gold or buried bullion is not clear. What is clear however is that when ground radar scans were conducted in 2008 the results showed traces of a metal much more dense than that of copper suggesting it was in fact gold.

I dowsed this area in 2006, and found a concentration of gold auras in one particular place shown on the following page. The interesting thing about this location is the same area where Mr Heinz-Peter Haustein the Mayor of the village had started his investigation in 2008.

The Nazis used to mark treasure tunnels and locations with a squared number 8. This number was found inside one of the tunnel systems that had been blown up by the Nazis near the end of the war very close to this area of Deutschneudorf. The number 8 was again repeated by the planting of trees very close to the Nazi treasure horde.

The squared "8" number can clearly be seen by the air, and would have been spotted by the Luftwaffe during WWII, where I believe treasure laden aircraft would have landed close by to unload more gold and taken by the SS inside the copper mines 10-15 metres below into vaults and tunnels where the entrances were then sealed using dynamite in the closing months of the Second World War.

These trees that make up the squared 8 marker can help us determine whether or not the age of the trees match up with same 1940's timeline. This image can be seen on the Google Earth image taken the 31st of December 2000.
It is interesting to note that the Imperial Japanese Army used the same squared eight symbol to denote buried treasure sites in the Philippines, particularly on the large island of Mindanao.

By measuring the size of tree trunk girth, we can estimate their age and when they were planted. It maybe that the trees were planted by ex SS or Nazis just after the war to mark the location of the treasure site so that in years to come, and seen by returning aircraft this group could have returned in peace time to recover what was buried inside the old copper mine.

The Olbernhau-Grünthal–Deutschneudorf railway, also known as *Schweinitztalbahn*, was a standard gauge branch line that ran from Olbernhau to Deutschneudorf. The line was opened in 1927 and closed in 1969.

In 1944/1945 Wehrmacht units established a depot for stolen art at Deutschneudorf suggesting that trains would transport Nazi treasure to Deutschneudorf for storage inside the old copper mines.

The picture above shows the dowsed location of gold auras very close to the village of Deutschneudorf.

These gold auras are NOT from natural gold deposits as suggested by locals. These auras are coming to the surface from large stored items of gold, and silver which can be verified by proper excavation using the correct type of sub surface equipment. One of the tunnels was used by the Germans as a communications base during WWII. Will someone now verify my findings possibly a gifted dowser in Germany perhaps?

Latitude N	Longitude E
AU Here: 50°36'46.79"	13°28'09.83" 175 feet deep
T2: (AU 0.5 Ton, Silver): 50°36'36.35"	13°28'07.65" 100 feet down in tunnel complex
T1: (AU 200Kg): 50°36'35.29"	13°28'06.90" 100 feet deep
Art Work Tunnel Here: 50°36'36.65"	13°28'07.56" 95 feet deep
Tunnel Here: 50°36'35.83"	13°28'08.23" 110 feet deep

18. HMS Frigate Lutine, Vlieland Northern Holland

Whilst working in Holland in 2013 as a Senior Electrical Manufacturing Engineer for Fokker Elmo Bv. I was asked by a Dutch colleague if I could dowse for HMS Lutine, a ship lost between the islands of Vlieland and Terschelling, in Northern Holland.

In this chapter I tell you the reader the history of the ship and of course my dowsing findings.

During the Siege of Toulon, France on the 27th September 1793, the French authorities surrendered the naval dock yards, the city, the arsenal and the French Naval fleet to the commander of the British Fleet Vice Admiral Lord Hood. One of these French ***Magicienne*** class frigates was called the Lutine. She was acquired by the Royal Navy and commissioned as HMS Lutine.

HMS Lutine was used as an escort ship guiding other ships in and out the shoal waters around northern Holland.

On the ninth of October 1799 this British frigate was wrecked off the Dutch coast, between the islands of Vlieland and Terschelling.

270 souls were drowned, only one person survived the terrible storm that smashed the frigate to pieces that terrible night. Sandbanks that constantly move with mud flats and deep outlets of water running between the islands made navigation in these parts on Northern Holland tricky for any captain especially in the 18th century.

The wreckage of the Lutine was just another casualty in the long line of ship wrecks. The newspapers of the day confirmed this accident by writing that a strong gale caused the destruction of HMS Lutine. Captain Portlock, commander of the English Fleet at Vlieland wrote to the Naval Admiralty in London stating:

"Sir, It is with extreme pain that I have to state to you the melancholy fate of his Majesty's Ship Lutine, which ship ran onto the outer banks of the Fly Island Passage on the night of the 9th. instant heavy gales of wind from the NNW and I am much afraid the crew except one man, which was saved from the wreck, have perished...This man when taken up was almost exhausted. He is of present tolerably recovered, and relates that the Lutine left Yarmouth Roads on the Morning of the 9th instant, bound to Texel, and she had on board Considerable quantity of money."

The Lutine's Final Voyage

In October 1799 she was charged by the Navy to transport about £1.2 million in bullion and coin (equivalent in value to £106 million in 2016), from Yarmouth to Cuxhaven in order to provide Hamburg's banks with funds to prevent a stock market crash and, possibly, to pay troops in North Holland. In the evening of 9th of October 1799, during a heavy north-westerly gale, the ship under Captain Lancelot Skynner, having made unexpected leeway, was drawn by the tidal stream flowing into the Waddenzee, onto a sandbank in Vlie off the island of Terschelling, in the West Frisian Islands. There, she became a total loss. All but one of her approximately 270 passengers and crew perished in the breaking seas.

HMS Lutine Recovery Time Lines

1800: Robbé recovered a cask of seven gold bars, weighing 37 kilograms (82 lb) and a small chest containing 4,606 Spanish piastres. Over the 4th and 5th of September, two small casks were recovered, one with its bottom stoved in, yielding twelve gold bars. There were also other, more minor, recoveries, making this year the most successful of all the salvage attempts; however, the expenses of the salvage were still greater than the recoveries by 3,241 guilders.

1801: Although recoveries were made, conditions were unfavourable and the wreck was already silted up. By 1804 Robbé reported: *The part of the wreck in which one is accustomed to find the precious metals has now been covered by a large piece of the side of the ship (which had previously been found hanging more or less at an angle), thus impeding the salvage work, which was otherwise possible.* Salvage attempts appear to have been given up at this point.

1814: Mr Pierre Eschauzier was allocated 300 guilders for salvage by the Dutch King and recovered "8 Louis d'or and 7 Spanish piastres fished out of the wreck of the Lutine.

1821: Eschauzier put together a syndicate with the intention of using a diving bell manned by *amphibicque* Englishmen. However, Mr. Rennie, the engineer died that year; in 1822, the bell arrived at the end of June, but operations were frustrated by bad weather and silting-up of the wreck; at this stage the wreck was reckoned to be 1 metre (3 ft 3 in) under the sand. Although salvage attempts continued until 1829, little was gained and the bell was sold on to the Dutch navy. In 1835, the sandbank covering *Lutine* shrank and moved south wards, with the depth of water being 9–10 metres (30–33 ft) and desultory attempts at salvage were made. Further attempts to raise capital were largely unsuccessful.

1857: It was discovered by luck that "a channel had formed straight across the Goudplaat sandbank, leading over the wreck, now clear of sand but had also sunk further below the surface within the channel, the bows and stern, together with the decks and sides, had torn completely away, leaving only the keel with the keelson above it and some wooden ribs attached to it. Recovery work immediately recommenced, now using helmeted divers (*helmduikers*) and bell divers (*klokduikers*), the latter using a bell called the *Hollandsche Duiker* ('Dutch diver'). However, a large number of unauthorised salvors also displayed an interest, which led the Dutch government to station a gunboat in the area. Over the course of the season approximately 20,000 guilders-worth of specie was recovered.

1858: The salvage season was hampered by poor weather but yielded 32 gold bars and 66 silver bars. This ship's bell was also discovered in this year.

1859: It became apparent that the treasure had been stored towards the stern of the ship, and that the stern was lying on its side, with the starboard side uppermost and the port side sunk into the sand. This area, however, only gave up 4 gold bars, 1 silver bar, and over 3,500 piastres.

1860: The depth of the wreck had reached 14 metres (46 ft) and the quantity of salvage was declining. Nonetheless, over the four years of salvage work, half a million guilders had been recovered: 41 gold bars, 64 silver bars, and 15,350 various coins, and the syndicate paid a 136% return; attempts were finally ended in 1863 as the wreck again was lost to the tide, silt and sand.

1860 - 1889: Attempts at salvage are reported to have recovered 11,164 coins valued at $4,600.

1867: An inventor called Mr Willem Hendrik ter Meulen, proposed using a 'zandboor' ('sand drill'), *a device which forced water into the sandy sea bed in order to clear a way for a helmet diver* and signed a three-year contract, subsequently extended for another three years and then a further twenty years. The plan was that when the depth of water reached 7 metres (23 ft), the machine would be used to excavate the same depth of sand down onto the wreck.

Mr Ter Meulen bought a steel-hulled, paddlewheel-driven 50 horse power steam tug, ***Antagonist***. The engine was modified such that it could be disconnected from the paddlewheels and used to drive the centrifugal 'whirlpool' pump. The pump was capable of pumping water at a rate of 21.5 cubic metres per minute (760 cu ft/min), but tests showed that 1.5 cubic metres per minute (53 cu ft/min) was sufficient, and the 'zandboor' took only a couple of minutes to penetrate through to the wreck. It was also found that the sand did not collapse once the diver descended through the drilled hole into the cavity excavated by the machine.

Unfortunately, the wreck remained heavily silted up, with the depth of water varying between a high of 2 metres (6 ft 7 inches in 1873) to a low of 5 metres (16 ft in 1868 and again in 1884). However, Mr Ter Meulen was responsible for re-establishing the landmarks used for taking transits of the wreck site and for establishing its position:

Latitude: 53°20'35"N, Longitude: 5°01'34" E Note: it is interesting to note that as I write this book these co-ordinates given by Mr Willem Hendrik Ter Meulen are not too far away from where I dowsed the location of the wreck in May 2012. I was unaware of this GPS location at that time I dowsed for HMS Lutine treasure site location.

1886: A cannon was salvaged and presented by **Lloyd's** to **Queen Victoria**: it is now on display at **Windsor Castle**. Another was offered to the **City of London Corporation** and is on display at the **Guildhall, London**. Another cannon was passed to the Lloyd's sports club in Essex. More are on display in Amsterdam's Stedelijk Museum, and at least four are in Terschelling. A number of coins and small relics were recovered to the value of £700.

1891and 1896: A few small coins were found, and cannon was presented to Queen Wilhelmina of the Netherlands from the Lutine wreck site.

1898: Two hundred weight of timber was recovered from which a chair was made for Lloyd's of London.

1911: A salvage company was organized to salvage the reported treasure from the Lutine.

1912: The same salvage company reported to have recovered silver coins, cannon, cannonballs, grapeshot and an anchor but no treasure.

1913: Two bow anchors, each weighing 3,900 kilograms (8,600 lb) were recovered and put on display in Amsterdam. Reportedly the outbreak of World War I prevented another salvage attempt.

1933: An attempt was made to salvage the reported treasure, but was stopped when the salvage bell was wrecked by a World War I sea-mine.

1934: an attempt was made to salvage the reported treasure.

1938: an attempt was made to salvage the reported treasure. Only one gold bar was found.

Note: As, in 1838, the complete archive of Lloyds was destroyed by fire, it is not possible to know how much exactly was on board ***HMS Lutine***.

If the estimation of £10 Million pounds sterling is to be believed, then there must still be a huge fortune at the bottom of the sea awaiting discovery.

Wind, Strong Currents Hamper Salvage Attempts

Wind, tide and strong currents can delay and hamper diving recovery operations. In no time the remains of the Lutine were covered with sand. And nothing in the Waddenzee ever stays in one position. Sandbanks, even the islands themselves, are continuously on the move. So the ship was really lost, for a long, long time.

Modern archaeological research has showed that, within a few hours after the ship ran aground, the rear part of the hull broke off and drifted away, with wind and currents in south-easterly direction and ended up at the south side of Vlieland, alone and forgotten, until now.

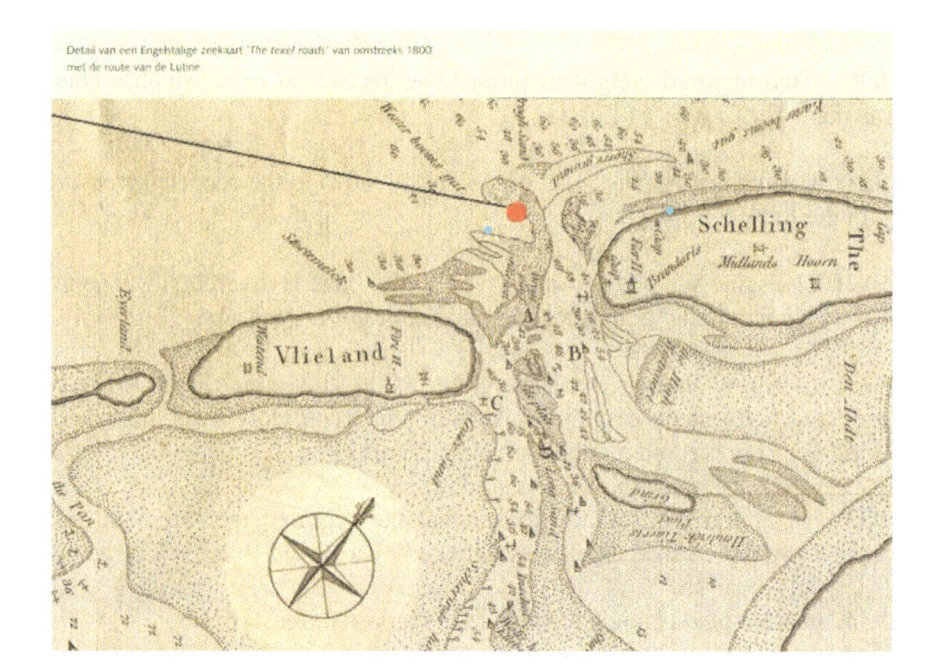

The map above shows where **HMS Latine** sank (shown in Red) and the position of where the two parts of the ship now lie (shown in blue).

A Wreck Divers Nightmare

Perhaps the best reason is found in an account by New Zealand diver Steve McIntyre who was on the 1980 salvage attempt: "It was the only diving job I remember when your fellow divers would not take your turn for you. When we left, none of us was ever going to go back there again".

Below is the Google Earth™ image showing the positions dowsed by the author on the 19th of May 2012 whilst I was working as a contractor in Holland. The constantly shifting sands mean that the positions of the wreck have divided, and the treasure hoard has scattered. Here we can see four gold targets even though I dowsed five gold locations. The gold bullion and coins are scattered by winds and tides across the sea bed over the past 218 years.

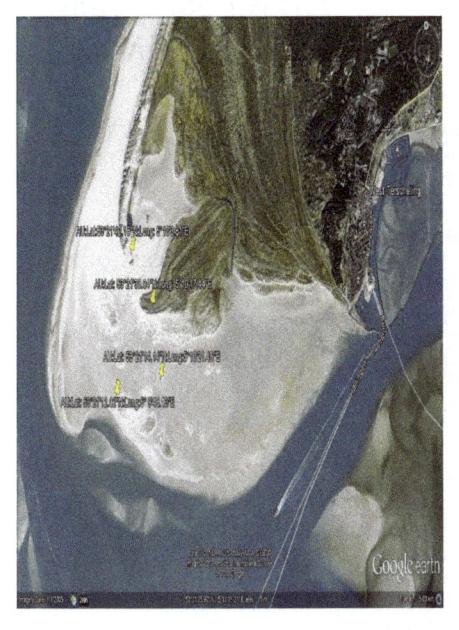

Latitude N	Longitude E
53°19′41.13″N	5°11′56.27″ E
53°21′30.04″N	5°10′17.44″ E
53°21′14.14″N	5°10′21.46″ E
53°21′42.16″N	5°10′03.81″ E
53°21′12.02″N	5°09′46.13″ E

Above: A closer look at the four gold targets (above). Below Are the GPS locations very close to where Mr Willem Hendrik ter Meulen said the Lutine was found in 1867 namely:

Latitude: 53°20′35″N, Longitude: 5°01′34″ E

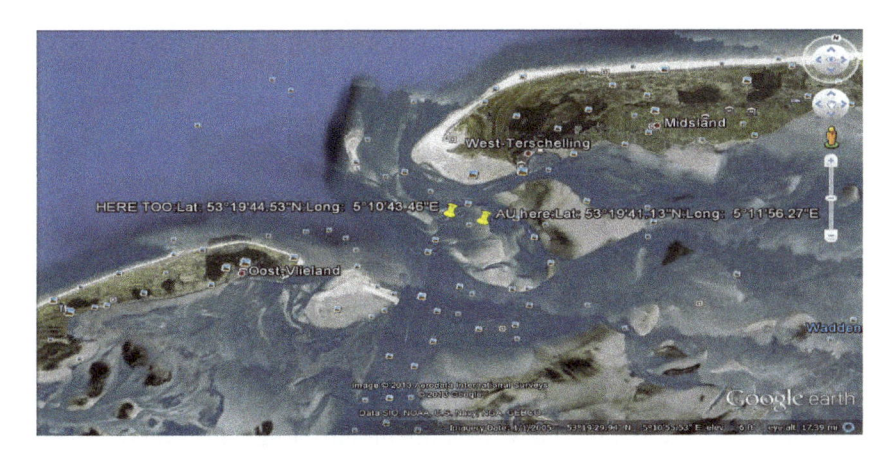

A Practical Recovery Solution:

In order to recover the remaining gold and riches laying inside the wreck a dive salvage operation must now use sand blowers and the use of a HDW1 600 ton salvage grab made by Smit Salvage based in Rotterdam to recover the wreck, and bring it up onto a salvage barge.

HDW1 600 Tonne Salvage Grab.

The SMIT debris grab 'HDW1' has been put into action successfully for many wreck removal projects during its respectful 30 years of age. It is one of the biggest salvage debris grabs in its class with a net grabbing capacity of 600 tonnes. Originally built as a conventional salvage debris grab with mechanical means (wire ropes) for closing the grab, the grab has been given a complete lifetime extension in 2007, including an innovative conversion of the mechanical wire rope system into an electrical-hydraulic actuation of the grab which increases the grabbing force.

(Photo rights Smit Salvage: See Appendix Smit Salvage).

Technical Specifications

Weight in air: 250 tons
Grabbing capacity: 600 tons
Hoisting speed: 60 - 90 metres/hour
Maximum grabbing force: 300 to 900 tons
Website: www.smit.com

It would make sense that the main two parts of the ship are located, and recovered from the sea bed using this giant grab shown above. This would ensure that the majority of existing treasure on board the wreck and the surrounding debris area is recovered and brought ashore on a salvage barge for all to see in a museum similar to that of the *Mary Rose*. Henry VIII's flag ship now on public view in Portsmouth, England, where 19,000 artifacts have been recovered from the wreck.

See: http://www.maryrose.org/

19. Monte Sorrate Nazi Treasure in Italy

The mountain village of San Oreste lies north of Rome and rests at the base of Monte Soratte. The mountain is honeycombed with mine shafts. On the 3rd of May, 1944, Nazi SS troops went to Monte Sorrate and in a rock-hewn vault deep within one of the many tunnels hid a fortune worth $72,000,000 USD.

The cache consisted of 60 tons of gold bullion seized by the German SS from the National Bank of Italy, plus a huge amount of jewelry looted by the Nazis from Rome's Jewish community. After depositing the treasure deep in the mountain, they then buried it under thousands of tons of rock with a huge explosion.

The lone survivor of this burial escaped only to be sought out and killed later on. Numerous treasure expeditions have sought this hoard without success. Until now that is! Below I give the dowsed location of where the gold aura is seeping out of the rocks.

Target location: **Latitude: 42°14'36.84"N Longitude: 12°30'12.22"E**
120 feet deep, Elevation: 646 metres.
Dowsed by the Author: 4th September 2010.

20. Adolf Hitler's Wolf's Liar Treasure in Poland

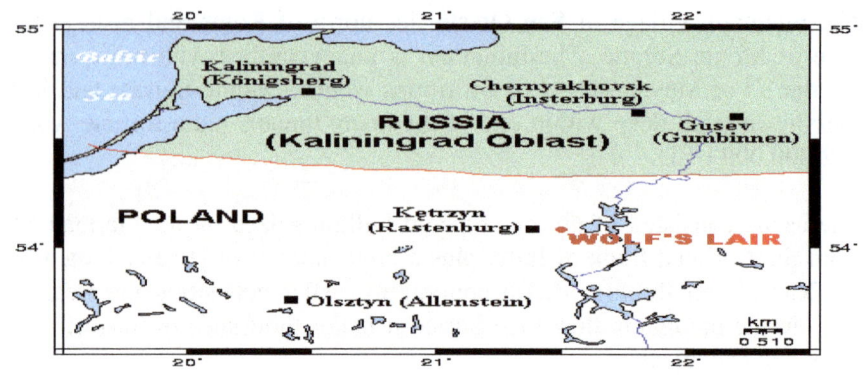

(See: **http://en.wikipedia.org/wiki/File:WolfsLairMap.png**).

In the very heart of Mazurian forests, about 8 kilometres (5.0 mi) from the small East Prussian town of Rastenburg, now Kętrzyn in Poland, we can still find the ruins of Adolf Hilter's war headquarters.

Wolf's Lair is the English name for Wolfsschanze, Adolf Hitler's first World War II Eastern Front military headquarters, **one** of several *Führerhauptquartier* (**Führer Headquarters**) located in various parts of Europe.

The place was a secret hidden military town built on the 21st June 1941 in the forest consisting of 200 buildings: shelters, barracks, 2 airports, a power station, a railway station, air-conditioners, water supplies, heat-generating plants and two tele-printers. In 1944 more than 2000 people lived here and on July 20th, 1944 Count Claus Schenk Von Stauffenberg made a failed assassination attempt to kill Adolf Hitler.

This complex was originally built for Operation Barbarossa, the 1941 German invasion of the Soviet Union.

Among those who were residents and worked here were: Adolf Hitler, Hermann Goring, Heinrich Himmler, Martin Bormann, Wilhelm Keitel, Joseph Goebbels, Dr. Fritz Todt, Albert Speer and other high ranking Nazi generals and officers. The original bunker system was constructed by Hochtief AG Organisation Todt**,** alas the later planned enlargement was never finished and the expansion work was stopped only a few days before the Russian advanced to Angerburg (now Węgorzewo), only 15 kilometres (9.3 miles) away.

Adolf Hitler first arrived at the Wolf's Lair late on the night of 23rd of June 1941 and departed for the last time on 20th of November 1944. Overall, he spent over 800 days there during that 3 $\frac{1}{2}$ year period.

The concreted complex was blown up and abandoned on 25th January 1945, but many of the bunkers were so thick that their damaged walls and ceilings remain. The historical buildings are located in Poland in the hamlet of Gierłoż (**German**: *Forst Görlitz*) near Kętrzyn.

Ten days after the start of the Red Army's *Vistula–Oder Offensive*. Despite the use of tons of explosives, one bunker required an estimated 8,000 kg (18,000 lb) of TNT.

The Red Army captured the abandoned remains of the *Wolfsschanze* on the 27th of January without bloodshed, the same day that **Auschwitz** was liberated further south. It took a further **ten years** until 1955 to clear over 54,000 land mines that surrounded the *Führerhauptquartier* installation.

Historical Visitor Site

Today the site is owned by the Polish Government and since the fall of Communism in the early 1990's the Wolf's Liar has been marketed as a tourist attraction. Visitors make trips from Warsaw or Gdańsk to see the once infamous Wolfsschanze, Adolf Hitler's first World War II Eastern Front military headquarters.

My Dowsed Search Findings

I decided that I would start my search for buried gold and items in the forest that surrounds the wooded area of the Wolf's Lair and then I would dowse a map of the Wolf's Liar showing the majority of the main buildings supplied by Wikipedia, the free encyclopedia on-line to see if I could locate any gold auras under the bunkers and buildings that make up the *Führerhauptquartier* installation. My findings can be seen on the following page.

Latitude N	Longitude E
AU Here: 54°04'52.83"	21°29'31.56" 25 feet deep

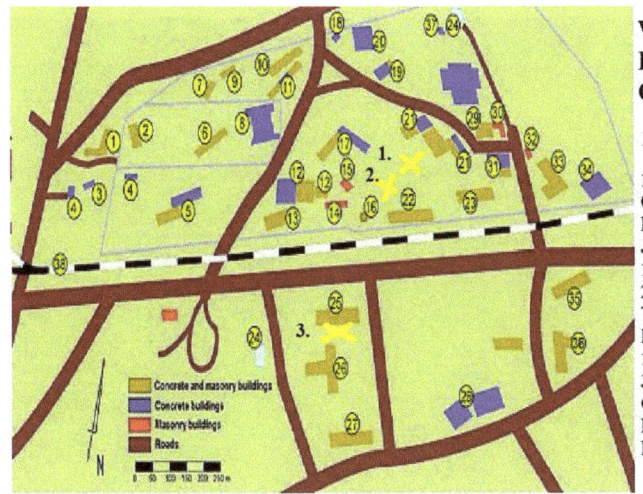

WOLF'S LAIR LAYOUT MAP OF BUILDINGS

DOWSED TARGETS

1. MIXTURE OF GOLD ITEMS RINGS, WATCHES, JEWELRY HERE 18 FEET DOWN
2. GOLD FROM TEETH AND GOLD RIMMED SPECS 18 FEET DOWN
3. 200Kg GOLD COINS 22 FEET DOWN MINT ROOM HERE

BUILDINGS KEY TABLE

1. Office and Barracks of **Hitler's bodyguard** 2. **RSD command centre** 3. Emergency generator 4. Bunker 5. Office of **Otto Dietrich**, Hitler's press secretary 6. Conference room, site of the **20th July 1944 assassination attempt** 7. RSD command post 8. Guest bunker and air-raid shelter 9. RSD command post 10. Secretariat under **Philipp Bouhler** 11. Headquarters of **Johann Rattenhuber, SS** chief of Hitler's security department, and Post Office 12. Radio and Telex buildings 13. Vehicle garages (The exact locations of buildings do not match this listing according to Wikipedia).	14. Rail siding for **Hitler's Train** 15. Cinema 16. Generator buildings 17. Quarters of **Morell, Bodenschatz, Hewel, Voß, Wolff** and **Fegelein** 18. Stores 19. Residence of **Martin Bormann**, Hitler's personal secretary 20. Bormann's personal air-raid shelter for himself and staff 21. Office of **Hitler's adjutant** and the **Wehrmacht's personnel office** 22. Military and staff mess II 23. Quarters of General **Alfred Jodl**, Chief of Operations of **OKW** 24. Firefighting pond 25. **Office of the Foreign Ministry** 26. Quarters of **Fritz Todt**, then after his death **Albert Speer**	27. RSD command post 28. Air-raid shelter with Flak and MG units on the roof 29. Hitler's bunker and air-raid shelter 30. New tearoom 31. Residence of General Field Marshal **Wilhelm Keitel**, supreme commander of OKW 32. Old Teahouse 33. Residence of Reich Marshal **Hermann Göring** 34. Göring's personal air-raid shelter for himself and staff 35. Offices of the **High Command of the Air Force** 36. Offices of the **High Command of the Navy** 37. Bunker with Flak 38. **Ketrzyn** railway line

Location: Latitude: 54° 4'.779"N Longitude: 21° 29'.619"E

My Dowsed Location of Gold Aura shown above (2Ton at 45ft.)
at Mamerki (Mauerwald): 9.40 miles
(15.12 Km) NNE of Wolf's Lair Location:

Location: Latitude: 54°11′6.64″N, Longitude: 21°38′13.57″E

According to Noel Richards, an historian, in a wooded forest called Mauervald (now **Mamerki,** Poland) during World War II, the German SS buried thousands of land mines throughout the area. Somewhere in this maze was the secret entrance to the Wolfschanze or Wolf's Den, the eastern front headquarters of Adolph Hitler. It is said that there is a secret "bank" in this region where an immense Nazi treasure of immense value still lies hidden containing gold, diamonds, rubies, emeralds, sapphires, platinum, all looted from thousands of churches, museums and banks in every occupied country and vast riches accumulated from millions of concentration camp victims. The secret underground city also is said to have included a mint. Will someone now verify my dowsed locations of buried Nazi loot recover it and give back to the relatives left behind when members of their families were murdered by the Nazis during the dark days of the Second World War.

21. The Zbiroh Castle Nazi Hidden Treasure in the Czech Republic

(Source: http://www.hotel-chateau-zbiroh.com/photos.htm)

Zbiroh Castle, is today known as Zbiroh Chateau and is located in the picturesque landscape of the Křivoklát Forest just 20 minutes travel time from Prague. Zbiroh is the first stately home in the Czech Republic and was mentioned in church chronicles at the end of the 12th century. Over the past centuries the castle was converted into the present neo-renaissance chateau. Famous owners have included King Ottokar II and the Emperors Charles IV, Sigismund and Rudolph II, which is why it is known today as the Three Emperors' Chateau, and is a thriving hotel where guests can stay in luxury and splendor.

Possible Hidden Nazi Treasure Down The Well?

An Article written by Chris Jarrett for the Prague Radio (Radio Praha) on the 19th of May 2006 stated that historians have been investigating the deepest water well in Europe, and finding some fascinating artefacts from the past history of the castle.

During the Second World War the Castle was taken over by the German SS communications division who set up a radio listening station that monitored the Allies radio communications from all over the world. The SS was originally attracted to the site by the veins of the semi-precious stone jasper which runs beneath Zbiroh. The Nazis discovered that jasper

reflects radio signals, and as such the site was a useful tool in monitoring radio traffic, and so set up their headquarters in the castle.
In 1965, military scuba divers, who discovered a chest of Nazi documents, suspected to be secret SS war records. Since then, further explorations have yielded similar documents.

Ms Maria Slavkovska, from the SCSA Security Company, responsible for the excavations, explains about the ongoing work:

"We have taken out 43 metres of backfill made up from very different sorts of material, like stone, dirt, metal and wood. One thing that was particularly special was a collection of old guns from the 17th century, or maybe older. We found some old documents from the SS German army, and when we open up the whole well we hope that we will find something older."

In addition to these finds, 163 metres below the chateau itself, investigators have recently discovered a false concrete bottom to the well, which, historical documents suggest, conceals a passageway used by the Nazis to store valuable stolen treasure. The false bottom was built from reinforced concrete and was decorated with jasper stones, which are common to the area, so that it looked natural. But further examination of the well may prove risky as the Nazis may have protected the cavity with explosives, either to secure the treasure or to prevent access to the chateau through the passageway.

"When we were cleaning it, we found some hand grenades which were explosive and we think that they tried to close the whole well by using them. Now there are special teams which will see if there is anything there which might explode, as the German army was not stupid; when they wanted to close something so that no one could get in, they would do it very professionally. So now we are doing everything we can to see if there are any dangerous items."

Another historical source stated:

"We know from witnesses that a Nazi aircraft landed close to **Zbiroh Castle** *and large cases were unloaded and taken towards it. We know that the last SS Garrison fled on foot without their uniforms and without taking anything. No one has found any trace of the cases and no one knows what was inside them." The castle has a series of tunnels and secret passages but closed off behind cement and possibly booby trapped by the Nazis before they fled during the closing months of the war"*

My Dowsed Findings

On the 29th Of December 2016, I decided to map dowse the castle building itself for gold and did not find any presence of a gold aura. I did however detect a very large gold aura situated to the south of the castle inside a small forested area.

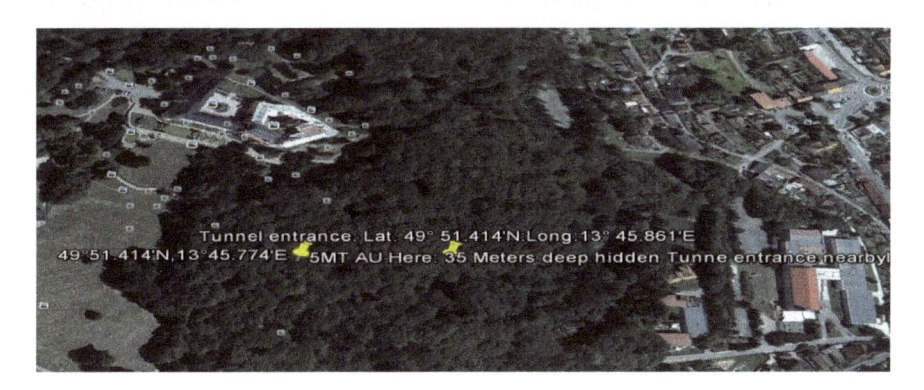

Gold Here: Latitude: 49°51'.414"N   Longitude: 13°45'.774"E
Tunnel Here: Latitude: 49°51'.417"N   Longitude: 13°45'.861"E

There is a tunnel complex inside the forested area. The entrance is well hidden but the size of the entrance means that trucks could have driven inside. The closed tunnel is to the right of the gold deposit shown above. The entrance is some 105 metres away. The amount of gold and other riches stored here is substantial, and stored inside a long tunnel that is at least 350 metres long and 35 metres below the forest floor.

I also picked up death around this treasure horde, after all it is looted riches from banks and Jewish people who were murdered by the Germans during WWII. These riches are covered in the blood of the innocent and I personally would not want to have anything to do with its final recovery. I estimate the gold buried here to be five metric tons of various sorts of gold bars, and gold jewelry, especially gold watches, gold rings, and gold necklaces.

I hope that someone can verify that there was once an old railway or Jasper mining tunnel here in the forested area where I pick up a massive gold aura. I believe that the tunnel entrance was closed by an explosive charge after the SS had hidden the stolen loot. This is the closed entrance to where the gold and riches will be found. Find a pile of old logs and the old tunnel will be found close by the GPS co-ordinates I have supplied.

It is also interesting to note that the small private road that leads up to the castle runs through the same small forest I have detected the massive gold aura in. Could it be that the SS high command had trucks unload vast riches inside the old tunnel at the dead of night and concealed by the darkness of the forest? As I write this book no one has reported to the Prague radio station that historians digging the old castle well have found anything that resembles hidden gold looted during the SS Nazi occupation of Zbiroh Castle.

22. Superstitions Mountains Lost Dutchman Gold Mine Location Arizona USA

In Arizona's Superstition Mountain range an ancient volcano towers high above the desolate landscape, a landmark to prospectors and treasure hunters from around the world.
It is called Weaver's Needle, and holds the key to the richest and most famous treasures in the history of the old American West.

In the year 1540, when a Spanish Conquistador called Francisco Vasquez de Coronado was part of a team of soldiers looking for another treasure, known as *"The Seven Golden Cities of Gold"*, also known as the hunt for Cibola. The expedition was known as the Coronado 1540 expedition.

Coronado's men were travelling past the superstitions mountain range when they heard from the local Apache Indians that the mountains are considered sacred by the tribe. The native Indians told the Spaniards that if they dare stray onto the sacred ground their Thunder God would take revenge upon them, causing tremendous suffering and horrible deaths.

The greedy Spaniards ignored the warnings when one of the Apaches mentioned that the mountain range held rich deposits of gold bearing ore.

According to historians it didn't take long for the expedition to find the gold deposits, but their joy soon turned to fear when soldiers began to mysteriously disappear and orders were given to the men never to stray more than a few feet away from the rest of the group. More of them continued to vanish, their bodies were found mutilated and their heads cut from their bodies.

Eventually the Spanish conquistadors left, refusing to return to the mountain, which they dubbed *Monte Superstition* meaning: "Superstition Mountain".

In 1748, the Superstitions range as well as 3,750 square miles of what is now Arizona, were given to Mexican cattle-baron, called Mr Don Miguel Peralta of Sonora, in a land grant.

Peralta discovered a rich gold mine and soon he was shipping millions of pesos in pure gold back to Sonora.

During the next century the Peralta family and their laborers would make periodic forays into Arizona, bringing out rich loads of ore. However, aware of the Apaches' mounting displeasure, they kept these mining trips to a minimum, not wanting to risk the wrath of the native Indians.

In 1847, the Mexican War (1845-1848) was raging and it looked as if Arizona might soon became part of the United States, so one of Don Miguel Peraltas descendants, Pedro, led a contingent of 400 men to the Superstition Mountains. The Spanish miners travelled to the mountain range hoping to excavate as much gold ore as possible before the mine was deemed to belong to the new American territory of Arizona.

The subsequent desecration of the Apaches sacred mountain had angered the Native Indians like never before and they began raising a large war party to drive Pedro Peralta and his miners out of their territory.

Peralta was told about the future Apache attack and left with his men from the area of the mine. He packed up his mules and wagons loaded with gold ore ready for the journey back to Mexico. Pedro took elaborate precautions to conceal the entrance to the mine and to eradicate any trace that they had ever worked there. Early the very next day, he assembled his men and headed for home but none of them were ever seen again.

Does The Old Gold Dutchman Mine Exist?

It is said that Jacob Waltz had a rich gold mine deep in the rugged mountains east of Apache Junction. The story tells of a German prospector who made periodic trips into the Superstition Mountains and returned to Phoenix with quantities gold ore. Mr Barry Storm, an early author on the subject of lost gold mines, believed Waltz had found a rich mine abandoned by the Peralta family of Mexico. Other writers suggested it was gold hidden by the Apaches after they massacred Pedro and his group of Mexican miners.

Today some prospectors believe Waltz's mine and the Peralta family cache are situated geographically at the same place.

Mr Alfred Strong Lewis, in his manuscript, Rain God's Gold, theorized that Peraltas or Spaniards worked the rich goldfields four miles northeast of present day Apache Junction and were massacred by the Apaches as they were preparing to leave the area and return to Sonora in 1847. I dowsed the area and found no gold here.

According to research in the U.S. national, state, county and municipal records, Mr Jacob Waltz, was born near Oberschwandorf, Wuttenburg, Germany around the year 1810. No church baptismal records support this, but his age on several census records do. He immigrated to America around 1839, arriving first in New York City. Waltz then traveled to the goldfields of North Carolina and Georgia. He arrived in Meadow Creek, North Carolina hoping to strike it rich. The Meadow Creek area had been well established by the time Waltz arrived. Like many foreigners he had been misinformed about the area.

It was on July 19th, 1861, in the Los Angeles County Courthouse, Jacob Waltz became a naturalized citizen of the United States of America.

Waltz departed California in 1863, heading for the Bradshaw Mountains of Arizona Territory. He was one of the earliest pioneer prospectors in the Bradshaw Mountain area. Waltz's name appears on the Gross Claim which was filed in Prescott, Arizona Territory on September 21, 1863. His name also appears on a special territorial census taken in 1864.

In 1868 Jacob Waltz moved to the Salt River Valley and filed a homestead claim on 160 acres of land on the north bank of the Salt River. It is from here Waltz began his exploratory trips into the mountains surrounding the Salt River Valley. Waltz would have prospected every winter between the years of 1868-1886. Waltz died in Phoenix, Arizona Territory on October 25th, 1891, in the home of Julia Thomas. Clues attributed to Waltz, both during his lifetime and as a deathbed revelation, have not yet resulted in finding the source of his gold until now.

Many government documents support that Jacob Waltz lived in Arizona Territory from 1863-1891. Shortly after Jacob's death Julia Thomas, Rhinehart and Hermann Petrasch took a trip to the Superstition Mountains to locate Waltz's rich gold mine. After several weeks in these rugged mountains Thomas and the Petrasches returned to Phoenix empty handed and broke. With no funds Julia produced several fake maps and sold them hoping to compensate for her losses.

The Petrasch family hunted for Waltz's mine for the rest of their lives and Julia Thomas was the first searcher for the Dutchman's Lost Mine. The Dutchman mine legend grew may be largely attributed to Julia Thomas and P.C. Bicknell.

Many Arizona historians believed that Julia Thomas gave an interview to Pierpont C. Bicknell, a free lance writer and lost mine hunter, shortly after her return from the Superstition Mountains in September of 1892.

Pierpont C. Bicknell, may be responsible for the tale of the Dutchman's Lost Mine. P.C. Bicknell was the earliest writer to associate Weaver's Needle, the Peraltas and Jacob Waltz with the Dutchman's Lost Mine in his writing. Bicknell's first major article on the Dutchman's Lost Mine appeared in the San Francisco Chronicle on January 13th, 1895, revealing several clues to the location of the Dutchman's Lost Mine. These clues closely paralleled those to which Julia Thomas often referred too.

The two hundred and forty-two square miles of rugged terrain found in the Superstition Wilderness makes it a difficult task to systematically search or prospect the region. Most professional geologists will insist there is little geological evidence to suggest a rich gold deposit could exist in these volcanic mountains. Jacob Waltz, the alleged owner of the Dutchman's Lost Mine, claimed his mine was located where no other miner or prospector would search for gold. A recent US Geological Survey could possibly support this clue Waltz left behind.

The application of the mercury vapor test over the Superstition Wilderness Area found the region to be highly mineralized. The report is indicative of deep seated mineral deposits. Who knows for sure, maybe one of those highly enriched mineralized bodies reached the surface by way of an *intrusion*.

Intrusion Explained

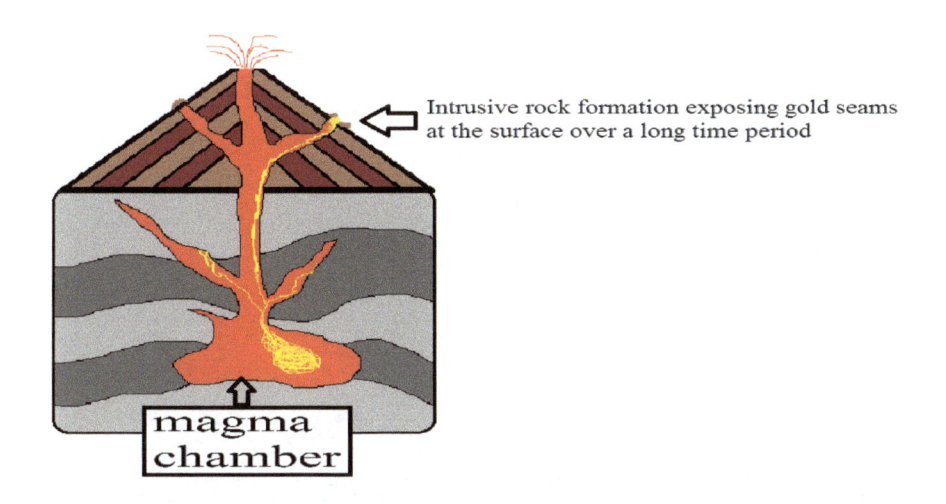

Intrusive rock formation exposing gold seams at the surface over a long time period

magma chamber

Intrusive rock forms within **Earth**'s **crust** from the **crystallization** of **magma**. Magma slowly pushes up from deep within the earth into any cracks or spaces it can find, sometimes pushing existing **rock** out of the way, a process that can take millions of years. As the rock slowly cools into a solid, the different parts of the magma, within this crystallization period quartz and gold layers can become exposed when the surrounding softer rock erodes away over time. It would make sense that such a gold/quartz layer would be found higher up the mountain ranges as the magna increased the size of the mountain range over millions of years.

This would explain why so many men could not find the Lost Dutchman's mine close to the valley floor. The location must therefore be higher on top of a mountain or very close the top where the sun, and wind erosion over hundreds of years had exposed an intrusion layer of quartz encrusted gold on the surface waiting for a miner to spot in the strong mountain sun light.

Prospectors and treasure hunters continue their search of this vast mountain wilderness for gold and lost treasure. Stringent rules for prospecting have limited their activity in recent years, but still they come to search for gold and lost treasure. The United States Department of Agriculture closed the Superstition Wilderness Area to mineral entry, at midnight, on December 31, 1983, to comply with the National Wilderness Act approved by Congress in 1964.

"The rays of the setting sun shine into the entrance of my mine. "It is also cannot be seen from the military trail, and is located in a north facing canyon!

Dowsed by the Author on: 28th May 2011.

The clues to Waltz's gold mine still ring clear through the towering peaks and deep canyons of the Superstition Wilderness Area.

"No miner will find my mine. To find my mine you must pass a cow barn. From my mine you can see the military trail, but from the military trail you cannot see my mine. The rays of the setting sun shine into the entrance of my mine. There is a trick in the trail to my mine. My mine is located in a north-trending canyon. There is a rock face on the trail to my mine."

Recently I found an article posted on the internet dated Friday the 20th Of November 2009 that stated Mr John V. Kemm from a place called Albuquerque New Mexico stated that he had found the Lost Dutchman's mine.

See Link: http://www.unexplained-mysteries.com/column.php?id=169267

Kemm states that by using the Peralta Maps he has the exact co-ordinates showing where the Lost Dutchman mine is located at GPS location:

Latitude: 33°26'46.06"N, Longitude: 111°21'44.38"W: 1847 m.

My original dowsed co ordinates dated 28th May 2011 say that the Lost Dutchman mine is located at GPS location:

Latitude: 33°26'13.55"N, Longitude: 111°24'33.73"W: 872.94 m.

I decided to map dowse the area around Mr John V. Kemm's co-ordinates and found a gold aura close by. These are my findings on 2nd of October 2016.

Gold Mine Here: **Latitude: 33°26'43.69"N, Longitude: 111°21'40.56"W: 1095.45 m.**

My original dowsed location made in 2011 is approximately 2.84 miles as the crow flies away from my second dowsed location made in 2016.

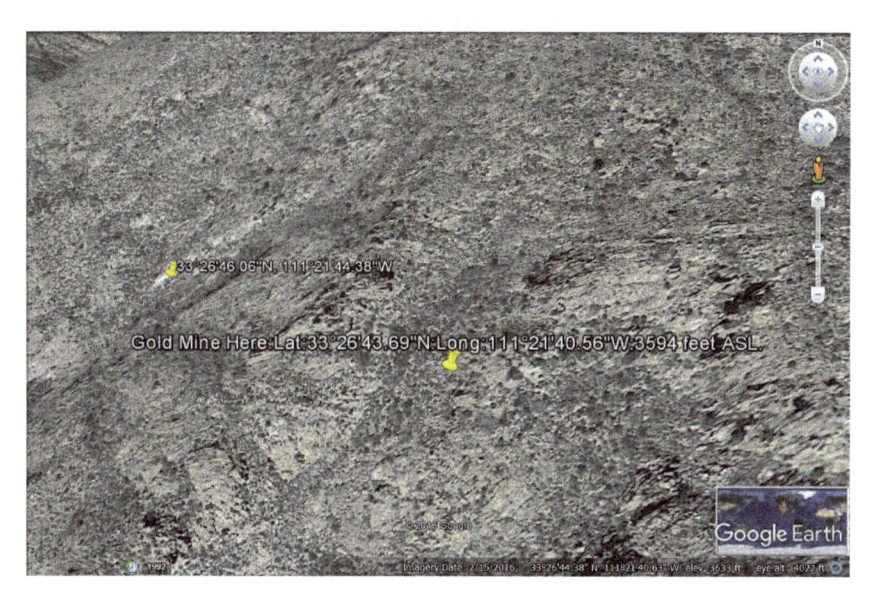

The picture above shows: Mr John V. Kemm: 33°26'46.06"N, 111°21'44.38"W: 1847 m. And my new dowsed gold aura location: 33°26'43.69"N, 111°21'.40.56"W: 1095.45 m.

I do not believe that there is gold at Mr John V. Kemm's location simply because I have dowsed the area around his target site and I did not detect any gold aura energy there.

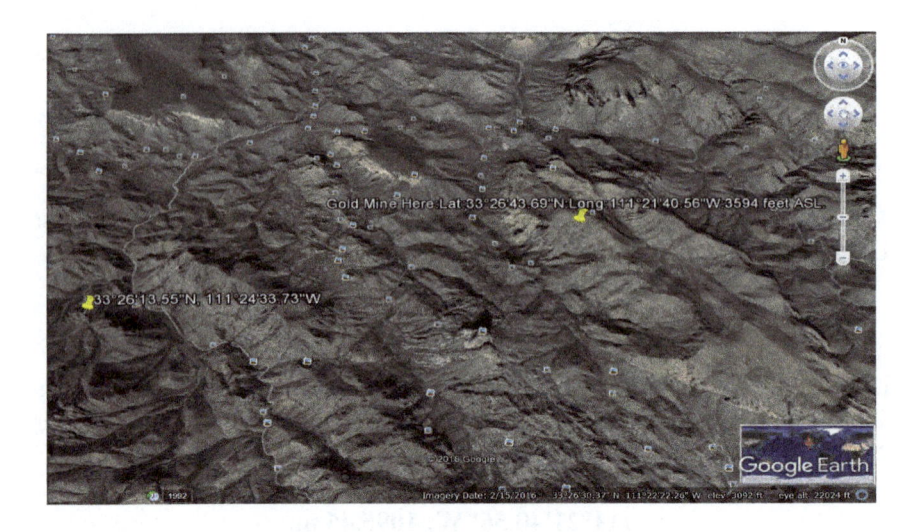

This picture above shows both of my dowsed locations for the Lost Dutchman mine. My original dowsed location made in 2011 is approximately 2.84 miles as the crow flies away from my second dowsed location made in October 2016, suggesting two gold deposits or mines.

Conclusion

The clues to Waltz's gold mine still ring clear through the towering peaks and deep canyons of the Superstition Wilderness Area. "No miner will find my mine. To find my mine you must pass a cow barn. i) From my mine you can see the military trail, but from the military trail you cannot see my mine. ii) The rays of the setting sun shine into the entrance of my mine. There is a trick in the trail to my mine. iii) My mine is located in a north-trending canyon. There is a rock face on the trail to my mine."

Both of these locations seem to match with Waltz's description, especially parts i, ii and iii.

The only conclusion that I can make from my findings and that of Mr John V. Kemm is that all three GPS locations must be investigated thoroughly. I would honour the wishes of the Apache tribe and keep well away, others will not. The quickest way to invest my findings without too much risk to life would be the use of a locally hired helicopter, from Papago Ahp Heliport in Phoenix AZ 35 miles west of my target GPS locations.
   See: http://www.phoenixhelicoptercharters.com/   Tel: 1-866-806-2456.

23. Locations of the Spanish Fleet Lost in the Great Hurricane of 1553-4 in Texas USA

In Veracruz, Mexico in the summer of 1553 a great fleet set sail for Spain, the twenty Spanish galleons carried 2,000 people returning to the motherland, loaded with gold, silver and casks filled with precious jewels, all plunder of the conquistadors. It was said to be the richest treasure fleet ever to sail from "New Spain" Mexico.

The armada of ships sailed across the Gulf of Mexico and stopped at Havana to refill their water casks, and to resupply with food for the long journey back to Spain. It is said that they left the safety of port under a yellow sky that warned of an oncoming storm. The fleet was suddenly caught in a hurricane, and several galleons sank under the waves while others on the edge of the storm managed to sail on up the eastern side of Florida. Only three ships managed to reach Spain half a year later and another one managed to limp back to Veracruz in Mexico.

The bulk of the fleet turned back across the Gulf to ride out the storm. The hurricane flung these galleons on the sands of Padre Island on the east coast of Texas in the general vicinity of a place later called Devil's Elbow.

Some of the ships were wrecked on the Isla Blanca, Texas. Three hundred survivors including priests, soldiers, sailors, women and children rested on the island. The men swam back to the wreckage to retrieve what they could. They found two crossbows and five quivers of arrows.

On the seventh day the survivors were attacked by native Indians called the Karankawas tribe and many of the Spanish were slaughtered. Some escaped into the surrounding sand dunes, protected by the soldiers with the two crossbows.

They fled down the island, with the Karankawas in full pursuit, shooting stone-tipped arrows at the fleeing survivors. The attacks continued as they struggled through the sands of the island, trying to reach Panuco, the most northern settlement in New Spain, near today's Tampico. Tampico is a city and port in the southeastern part of the state of Tamaulipas, Mexico. It is located on the north bank of the Pánuco River, about 10 kilometres inland from the Gulf of Mexico

Before they reached the tip of the island, all the women and children had been murdered. Fifty of the remaining men were killed at Brazos Santiago Pass estuary. (Latitude: 26° 3.954'N Longitude: 97° 9.519'W).

One Spanish friar called Marcos de Mena managed to survive the horrible trek and he told the story of what happened. Friar de Mena had been shot in the eye by an arrow and had six other wounds, he survived and made it to Mexico, based upon his tale of what happened, the authorities in New Spain decided to mount a salvage operation under the command of Angel de la Villafana to recover the lost treasure.

In the spring of 1554, the salvage fleet arrived. The ships were fitted out with grappling hooks and they brought Indian divers from Yucatan, famed for their ability to stay under the water for a long time.

There was even a crude diving bell. The fleet was met by Vasques, who knew where the ships went down and where the others broke apart. He helped guide the salvage operations.

The divers found silver and gold bars on the clay bottom. Casks and chests were brought up from wrecked hulls. Ship by ship, they reclaimed the king's treasure. When the salvage fleet returned to Mexico, in the summer of 1554, the share of the treasure awarded to Vasques was said to be as great as that of Villafana, the commander of the salvage fleet. But one of the wrecked galleons was never found.

In 1904, a Corpus Christi resident claimed he found an old Spanish ship off Padre Island. (Lat: 27° 28.038'N 97° Long: 17.788'W). Mr Alex Meuly said he found the remains of the galleon and estimated that it held more than a million dollars worth of gold. Was it the missing ship from the 1553-4 treasure fleet?

Mr Meuly said he found it in 17 feet of water, on a clay bottom, 420 feet from shore, and 35 miles down the island. "The treasure was of such magnitude," he wrote a friend, "I could scarcely believe my own senses."

He constructed a trailer to recover the treasure and intended to take it back to Corpus Christi. Sadly Meuly never found the ship again. Perhaps he had only a fleeting glimpse of the vessel, or in some way lost his bearings.

On the following pages I have supplied you the reader Google Maps™ of where the treasure wreck locations are to be found.

I have compiled a table here showing all of the GPS locations shown on subsequent pages in this chapter.

Latitude N	Longitude W
AU Target 1: 27°10'26.56"	97°25'47.35"
AU Target 2: 27°14'01.48"	97°24'10.63"
AU Target 3: 27°14'30.22"	97°23'49.35"
AU Target 4: 27°13'41.93"	97°25'03.63"
AU Target 5: 27°32'01.46"	97°17'21.49"
AU Target 6: 27°28'38.47"	97°17'21.41"
S.Wreck: 27°34'11.18"	97°15'53.42"

Check Here For Wreck: Lat: 27°20'54.90"N Long: 97°13'14.31"W

I decided to dowse for these lost Spanish vessels on the 26th June 2011, on following pages are the GPS locations of where I believe the Spanish ship wrecks are located today. The yellow pins are where I have detected a gold aura. Further dowsing will reveal the quantity of gold and the exact depth of the target.

Please seek the guidance and permission from the National Parks Service, Padre Island P.O. Box 181300 Corpus Christi, TX 78480.

See: https://www.nps.gov/pais/learn/historyculture/1554-1.htm
Also see: https://tshaonline.org/handbook/online/articles/etpfe

Dowsed by the Author: 26th May 2011
Ship Wreck Locations South of Padre Island, Texas.

Meuly stated that he found one wreck in 17 feet of water, on a clay bottom, 420 feet from shore, 35 miles down the island. "The treasure was of such magnitude," he wrote a friend,

"I could scarcely believe my own senses."

Note: Targets 1, 4, 2, and 3 are in this area and 35 miles south from Corpus Christi! This fact was found out **AFTER** I had dowsed these targets.

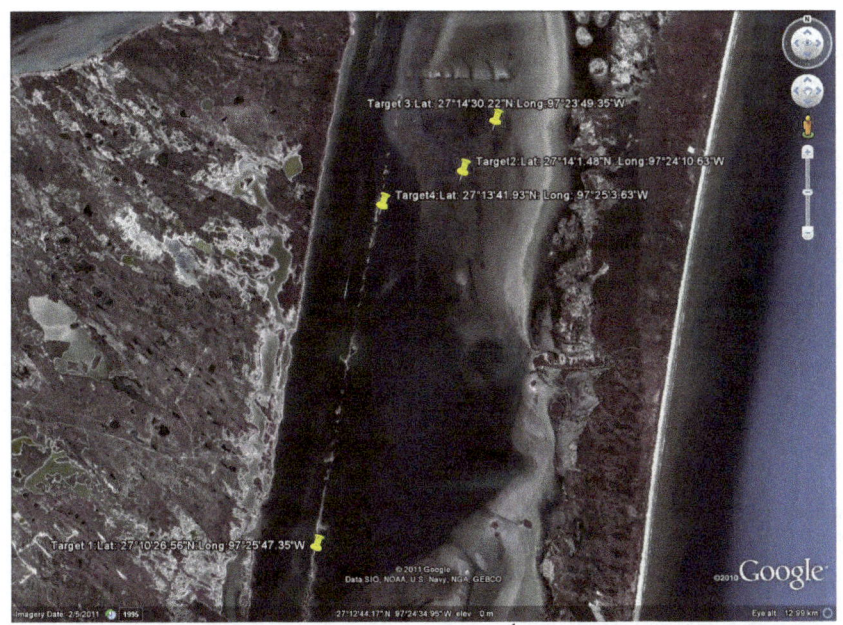

Dowsed by the Author: 26th May 2011

The ship wrecks containing gold are shown here behind the sand bar inside the lagoon area south of Padre Island, presumably washed there in the great storm surge of 1553/4.

Dowsed by the Author: 26th May 2011

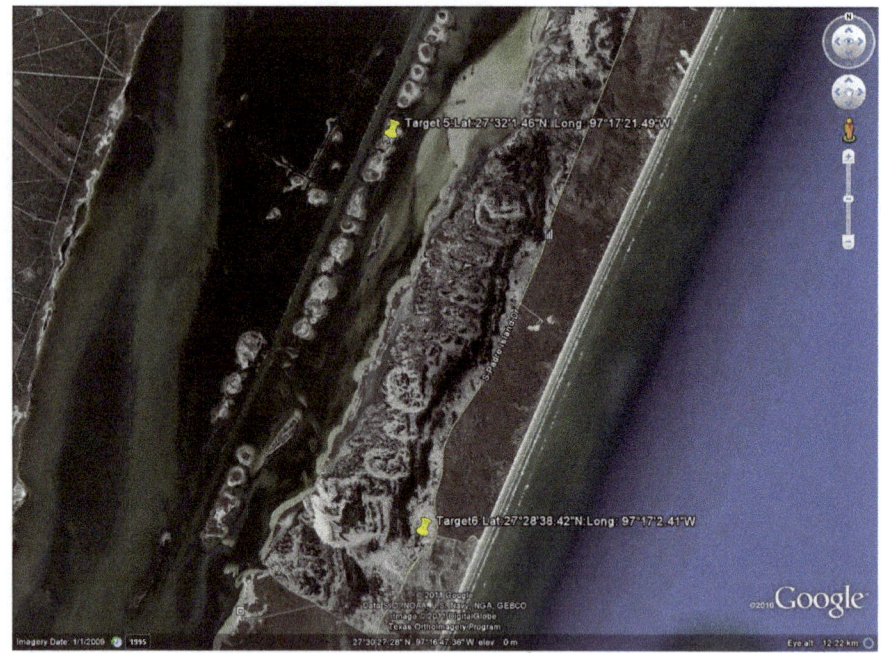

Dowsed by the Author: 26th May 2011

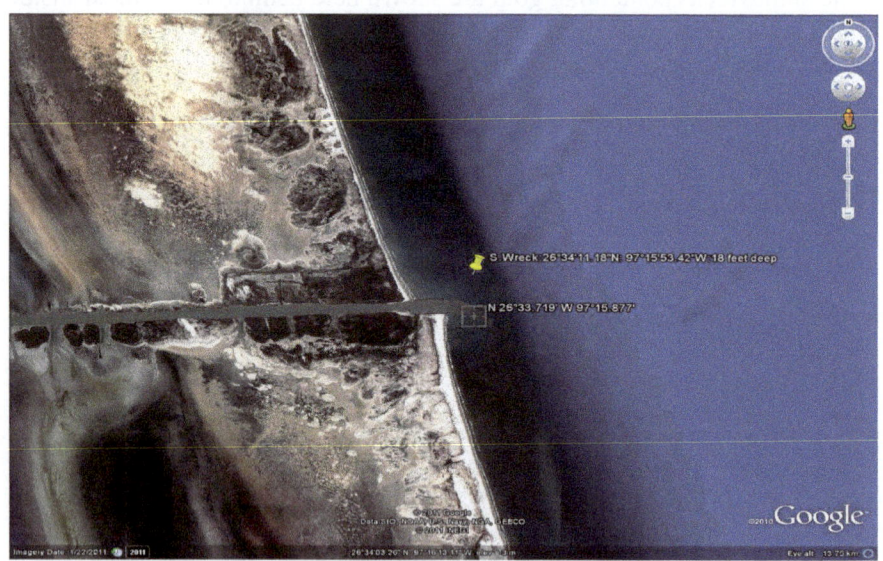

Dowsed by the Author: 26th May 2011

A ship wreck laden with gold coins lies here just off the Isla del Padre (Puerto Mansfield) Estuary entrance.

24. Poverty Island Treasure, Lake Mitchigan USA

Poverty Island is a small island in the U.S. state of Michigan. The island is within Delta County in Lake Michigan and is home to the Poverty Island Light Station, an abandoned lighthouse which is in disrepair. Poverty Island is currently owned by the federal government.

In 1863, when the tide of the United States Civil War was turning for the Union side, the south was desperate for cash, and asked France for financial help. According to the story the French Emperor, Napoleon Bonaparte III, secretly dispatched a sailing ship loaded with gold across the Atlantic to Canada. It sailed secretly down the St. Lawrence River and into Lake Michigan. But some believed that, while traveling inland to Chicago, the ship was attacked and sank. Others believe it was shipwrecked in a storm. Either way, the chests of gold never arrived.

The hunt for the fabled lost treasure in Lake Michigan near Poverty Island continues. For more than 149 years people had exhausted their savings looking for the King's ransom of gold worth between **$300,000,000** and **$450,000,000.**

Another Legend says that a 60ft schooner was carrying 5 chests of gold bullion supplied by France for use by the Americans in their fight against the British, and was wrecked off the island which is East of Wisconsin. The chests are valued at $400 million USD. There have been many attempts to locate it, well here it is!

Dowsed by the Author: 22nd June 2013

25. The Alamo Mission San Antonio Texas Treasure USA

(The Alamo drawn in 1854)

Many of us remember the 1960 film "The Alamo" produced and directed by Mr John Wayne and starring Wayne as Davy Crockett. The picture also starred Richard Widmark as Jim Bowie and Laurence Harvey as William B. Travis. The movie set was constructed near Brackettville, Texas, on the ranch of James T. Shahan. Chatto Rodriquez.

The real Alamo Mission however can be found in San Antonio, commonly called **the Alamo** and originally known as *Misión San Antonio de Valero*, is part of the **San Antonio Missions** in **San Antonio**, **Texas**, **United States**. Founded in the 18th century as a Roman Catholic mission and fortress compound, it was the site of the Battle of the Alamo in 1836.

In December 1835, during Texas' war for independence from Mexico, a group of Texan volunteer soldiers occupied the Alamo, a former Franciscan mission located near the present-day city of San Antonio. On February the 23rd, 1836, a Mexican force numbering in the thousands and led by:

General Antonio Lopez de Santa Anna (seen left) began a siege of the fort. Though vastly outnumbered, the Alamo's 200 Texican defenders commanded by Mr James Bowie and

Mr William Travis and including the famed frontiersman Davy Crockett, held out courageously for 13 days before the Mexican invaders finally overpowered them.

For Texans, the Battle of the Alamo became an enduring symbol of their heroic resistance to Mexican oppression and their struggle for independence, which they won later that year.

The Alamo was the sight of one of the most famous battles in American history, when 188 men, tried to fight off the powerful Mexican army of 6,000 well armed men. What most people probably do not know is the legend of a massive treasure of gold and silver said to be buried somewhere on the grounds of the Alamo.

A historical researcher and fortune hunter called Mr Frank Buschbacher, believe that in an effort to wage a revolution against Mexico and declare Texas independence, men like: James Bowie (seen left) who arrived at the Almo mission on January the 19th with orders to destroy the complex. But instead he appointed himself the garrison's co- commander. Together with Davy Crockett had actually brought millions of dollars worth of treasure to the Alamo. This money was meant to raise an army and pay for their oncoming war with the Mexican Army. The treasure was called the ***San Saba*** treasure and it was lost when all 188 men lost their lives in that famous battle. Those who believe the treasure exists think the men buried it beneath the compound. Others state that this treasure was buried at the San Saba Mission in Menard, Texas. Was the treasure transported from Menard to the Alamo mission by James Bowie and Davy Crockett and buried there?

Mr Buschbacher has excavated areas around the Alamo, one was the old water well used by the Texican soldiers during the battle. Mr Buschbacher believed that Col. Bowie had ordered that the treasure be dumped inside the old water well situated in the old Plaza near the Old Chapel located at the rear of the fort as the battle was waging but not a trace of gold or silver has ever been found.

(Left: Jim Bowie, or Santiago Bowie)

I have dowsed the Alamo area and the only dowsed detection of gold is outside the walls of the old convent yard at the rear of the chapel. I believe that there was an old miner's house on this site and that the gold was buried under the wooden foundations of this building for safe keeping.

I have marked the area with a yellow box on one of the old Almo maps of the time to show that the gold target was buried by James Bowie and Davy Crockett outside the convent yard walls very close to where the river splits into a Y shaped fork. I believe both men would have chosen this place in order to stop the Mexican Army finding the treasure inside the mission grounds if they had became overran by the attacking forces. The Mexican soldiers would have assumed that any treasure would have been stored inside the Alamo compound locked inside a strong room or storeroom guarded by Texan soldiers.

The use of Ground Penetrating Radar and a deep search metal detector will verify the existence of the gold in barrels burial sites in this location these are:

Au Here Latitude: 29°25'33.99"N Longitude: 98°29'8.83"W 14 feet.

Au Here Latitude: 29°25'34.19"N Longitude: 98°29'8.76"W 14 feet.

Au Here Latitude: 29°25'34.23"N Longitude: 98°29'8.74"W 12 feet.

Au Here Latitude: 29°25'34.2"2N Longitude: 98°29'8.84"W 11 feet.

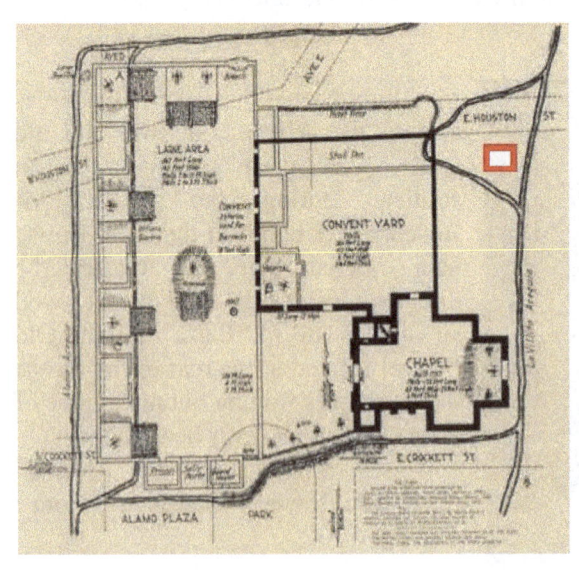

Left: A map showing the location of buried gold from the 1800's (Shown in red).

Below: A drawing of where the gold location is buried today at depths ranging from 11 to 14 feet.

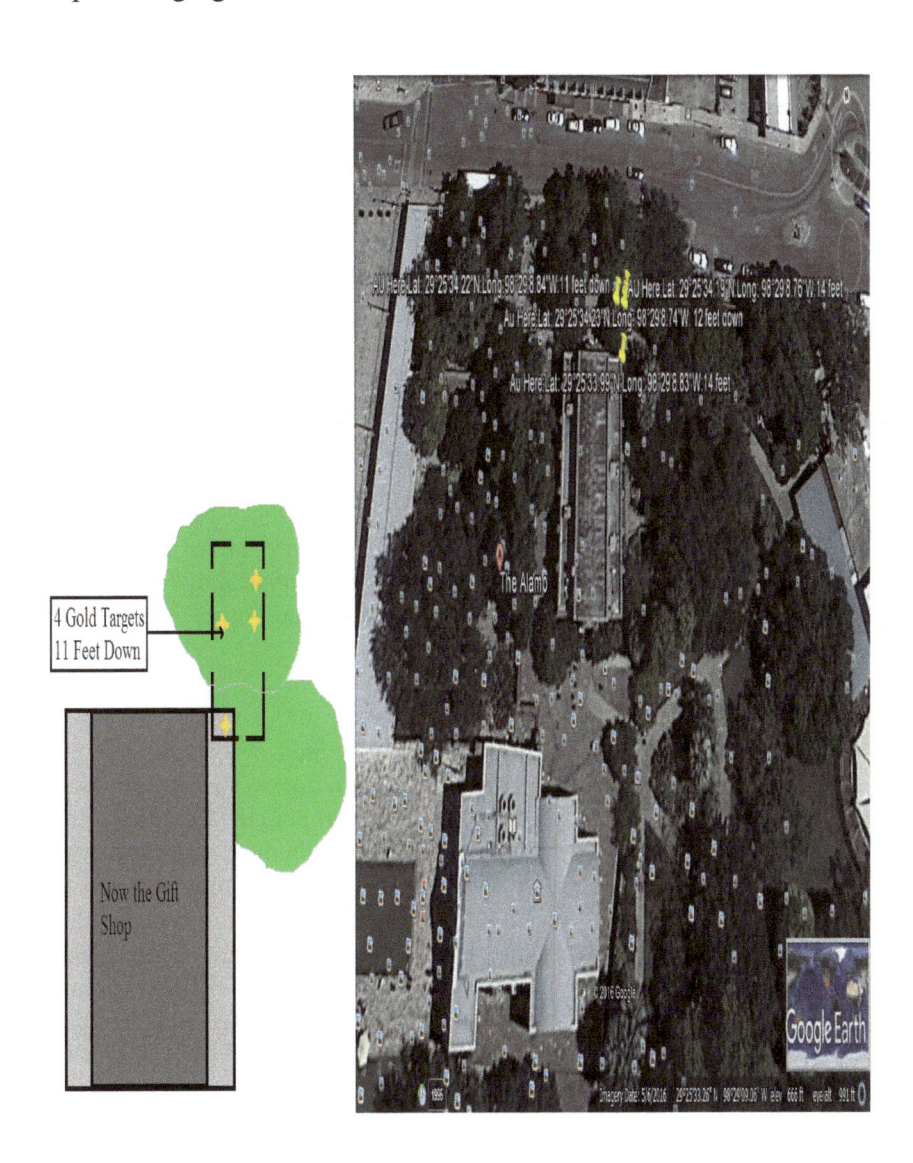

26. Atocha & Margarita Wreck Sites Key West Florida USA

Many treasure hunters have read or heard about the famous Spanish ship wrecks the Atocha and the Margarita.

Both these wreck were found by Mel Fisher of the coast of Florida Keys. For those of you who have not come across this fascinating story, then here is some history surrounding one of the biggest treasure recoveries in modern time.

On September the 4th, 1622, the Spanish galleon Nuestra Señora de Atocha set off from Havana, Cuba, with a flotilla of nine other ships bound for Spain. Loaded with a cargo of silver, gold, gems, and other New World riches.

The ships sailed into a violent hurricane as they made their way through the Florida straits the following day. It is said that hundreds of people drowned when the ships sank, including sailors, clergy, Spanish soldiers, slaves and members of the nobility. After searching for 16 years, in 1985 treasure hunter Mel Fisher unearthed the treasures of the Spanish galleon Nuestra Señora de Atocha north of Rebecca Shoal, Key West in sea water less than 40 feet deep.

A haul of gold bars, gold chains and rings were salvaged from part of the wreck debris field worth a staggering $400 million USD. What people don't know is that the Atocha wreck site has been scattered over the centuries that today covers a distance of 8 nautical miles of the ocean floor.

Today, the Mel Fisher diving and salvage team now headed by Mel's nephew, are currently still diving these wreck sites searching for rest of the ships manifest which includes hundreds of bars of silver, One Hundred Thousand silver coins, 60 lbs of Columbian Emeralds and at least eight 4,000 lb bronze cannons.

Here are my findings dowsed in 2012, and on the 1st of October 2016 shown below:

Latitude N	Longitude W
Silver Here: 24°37'17.82"	82°16'38.27"
	45 feet deep in sand
AU Coins Here: 24°35'19.42"	82°15'27.77"
	32 feet deep in sand
AU Here: 24°34'12.77"	82°15'17.59"
	32 feet deep in sand
AU Here: 24°34'11.45"	82°16'12.17"
	35 feet deep in sand
AU Here: 24°32'37.29"	82°19'16.73"
	40 feet deep in sand
AU Here: 24°34'53.28"	82°32'43.36"
	38 feet deep in sand
Emeralds Here: 24°36'59.76"	82°10'22.84"
	35 feet deep in sand
Cannon Here: 24°34'40.48"	82°17'20.19"
	33 feet deep in sand
San Miguel: 23°58'23.43"	81°36'22.26"
	40 feet deep in sand
Silver Here: 23°57'32.66"	82°41'27.26"
	35 feet deep in sand

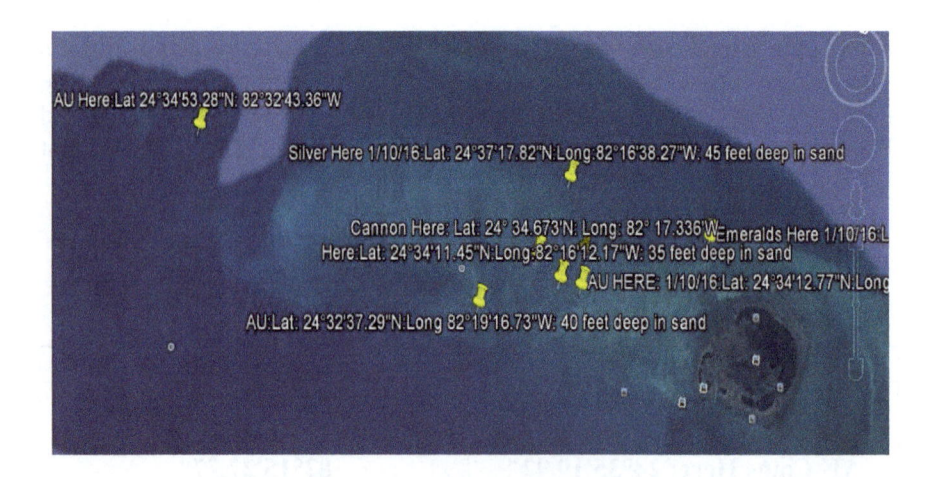

You can see the wreck debris field seems to be following in an S/W to an N/E direction.

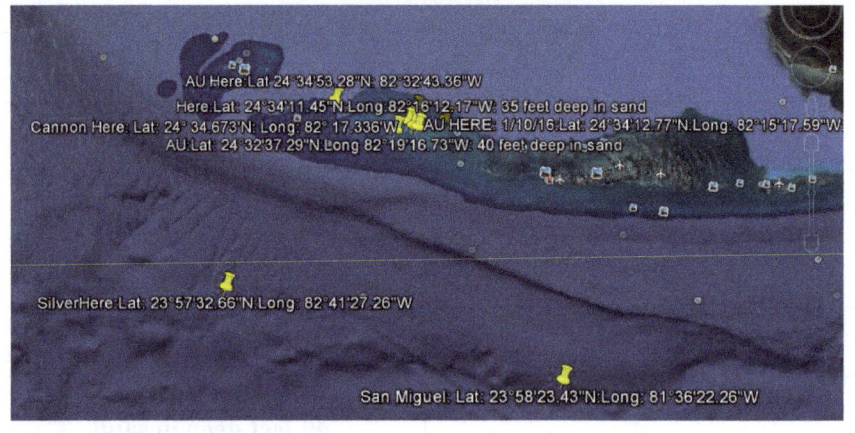

Conclusion

I hope that the current Mel Fisher team will look at my findings and compare my GPS locations with their own known treasure debris field to see if there is a correlation to my dowsed findings. I believe many of my dowsed targets match lost artefacts from the Atocha, but also I have identified other artefacts from other "unknown" shipwrecks lost in storms and hurricanes long ago. Further dowsing will be needed to identity the names of the ships lost in this area of Key West Florida.

See Links: http://melfisher.com/default.html and
http://www.melfisher.org/

27. Oak Island Treasure Locations Nova Scotia, Canada

Oak Island is a 140-acre (57 ha) island situated in Lunenburg County on the south shore of Nova Scotia, Canada. The tree-covered island is one of 360 small islands in Mahone Bay and rises to a maximum of 35 feet (11 metres above sea level).

This small island is the location of the so-called Money Pit, a site of numerous excavations to recover **treasure** believed by many to be buried there. The island is privately owned, and advance permission is required for any visitation rights to be granted to any budding treasure seekers. Several documented treasure recovery attempts have found layers of apparently man-made artefacts as deep as 31 metres, but ended in collapsed excavations and flooding. Critics argue that there is no treasure and that the pit is a natural phenomenon, likely a sinkhole. Excavations have nevertheless revealed evidence of man-made architectural structures and markings believed to been carved in rocks by the knights templar's.

Treasure Theories

There has been wide-ranging speculation amongst treasure hunters as to who originally dug the pit and what it might contain. Later accounts say that oak platforms were discovered every 10 feet (3.0 m) but the earliest accounts simply say that "marks" of some type were found at these places. They also say there were "tool marks" or pick scrapes on the walls of the money pit and that the dirt was noticeably loose and not as hard packed as the surrounding soil. One expedition said they found the flood tunnel at 90 feet, and that it was lined with flat stones. However, Mr Robert Dunfield (a trained geologist) wrote that he carefully examined the walls of the re-excavated pit and was unable to locate any evidence of this tunnel.

The cipher stone, which one researcher is said to have translated to read "Forty feet below two million pounds are buried", was allegedly last seen in the early 20th century.

The accuracy of the translation, whether the symbols as depicted maybe in question or if they meant anything at all still remains disputed. Barry Fell, noted author of 'America BC' and 'Saga America' was sent a copy of the inscription by the chief archivist of the Nova Scotia Archives in the late 1970s. Fell, who had previously translated coded writings on stones found elsewhere in North America, concluded that the symbols were similar to those used by an early Christian sect known as the Copts and when translated implied that the people needed to remember their God or else they would perish. Other theories suggest that there is indeed vast buried treasure awaiting discovery on Oak Island.

Pirates And The Navy

These wild theories claim that there is pirate treasure buried on Oak Island belonging to Blackbeard, or Captain Kidd. Others say that English, Spanish even French Sailors buried treasure on the Island. The author John Godwin suggested that the Money Pit was dug by the French army loot taken from the treasury of the Fortress of Louisbourg Novia Scotia and buried there. This theory is plausible since the British forces had captured the fort both in the years 1745 and then again in 1758. It certainly would make sense that the French would not want the British forces to also capture money and gold held by the French garrison.

Marie Antoinette's Jewels

The priceless jewels of Marie Antoinette (which are historically missing, save for some specimens in the collections of museums worldwide) on Oak Island. During the French Revolution, when the Palace of Versailles was stormed by revolutionaries in 1789, Marie Antoinette instructed her lady-in-waiting to take her prized possessions and flee. Supposedly, this maid fled to London with such royal items as Antoinette's jewels and perhaps other treasures, artwork or documents.

The tale then goes on to tell that this young woman fled from London to Nova Scotia, through the royal connections she would have had during her service to the queen at Versailles, she managed to contract the French navy to help construct the famed 'pit' on the island. This theory lacks any historical documentation. During the French Revolution would place the construction of the Oak Island structure very close to its initial discovery by Daniel Mc Ginnis in 1795. Whether such a complex engineering effort could have been completed in that small space of time (6 years) is feasible, though no official date of its construction exists. However, other theories do suggest the structure is indeed French and naval in style.

Other experts have stated that The Knights Templar buried the Holy Grail even the Ark of the Covent. Another crazy suggestion states that the Money Pit is the remains of a Viking Ship. If this was the case where did the Vikings get coconut fibres from? Surely not Norway!

Suggestions that the pit is a natural phenomenon, specifically a sinkhole or debris in a fault, date to at least 1911. There are numerous sinkholes on the mainland near the island, together with underground caves.

In 1949, workmen digging a well on the shore of Mahone Bay, at a point where the earth was soft, found a pit of the following description: "At about two feet down a layer of fieldstone was struck. Then logs of spruce and oak were unearthed at irregular intervals, and some of the wood was charred. The immediate suspicion was that another Money Pit had been found.

More recently, (October 2016) the History Channel has been filming the exploits of brothers Marty and Rick Lagina who have been working for the past eight years to uncover once and for all whether there is buried treasure on Oak Island. See: "The Curse of Oak Island".

Check out exclusive HISTORY content: Website: http://www.history.com

In episode 1 of season 4 of *The Curse of Oak Island*, a New York book author and researcher called Zena Halpern tells the search team that she has discovered that the Knights Templar visited an Island of Oaks between the years 1178 to 1180.

In a book she was given several years ago maps of the island and a cipher were found. She states that the gold buried on the island came from Africa transported possibly by the Templars. A French map dated 1347 shows the locations of various places on the island, including "The Oak Enter Here".

Background Notes

All these theories are interesting but were irrelevant when I dowsed Oak Island for the presence of gold auras and nothing else on the 27th February 2010.

The picture on the next page shows the locations of the various gold and historical treasure locations: Massive T" Location: "Expect markers or gold deposits at": 145,190 and 230 feet. Locations T1 and T3 "Expect markers or gold at: 17, 44, 70, and 150 feet. Location T2, gold deposit buried at 40 feet.

Oak Island Dowsed by the Author: 27th February 2010

Latitude N	Longitude W
T1: 44°30'47.44"	64°17'19.13" 150 feet deep
T2: 44°30'44.80"	64°17'15.83" 40 feet deep in sand
T3: 44°30'48.09"	64°17'18.24" 150 feet deep in sand
Massive Treasure: 44°30'49.89"	64°17'55.11" 160 feet deep in sand
Mother Load Treasure: 44°30'43.26"	64°17'36.81" 195 feet in shaft

Conclusion

It is interesting to note that locations T1 and T3 are very close the original Money Pit location which a local settler called Daniel Mc Ginnis found in 1795 with his two friends John Smith and Anthony Vaughan. The treasure hunters started to dig for Pirates Treasure that they believed to belong to Captain William Kidd. According to three sister's direct ancestors of Daniel, the three young men did find three chests full of gold and silver items at a depth of 90 feet.

These chests were shared equally just before the sea water came flooding in when a layer of oak logs were removed from the Money Pit shaft. Many believe that these three treasure chests were a "giveaway" and that the real treasure was located in a cavern some 190 plus feet down.

28. Yamashita Treasure Locations in the Philippines Operation "Golden Lily" (*Kin No Yuri*)

1937-1945 A Brief History

After Japan's full-scale invasion of China on 7th July 1937, Emperor Hirohito appointed one of his brothers, Prince Chichibu, to head a secret organization called Kin No Yuri "Golden Lily" (taken from one of the Emperor's poems) whose function was to ensure that all stolen *"war booty"* riches were to be properly accounted for. Putting an Imperial prince in charge guaranteed that everyone, even the most senior commanders, would follow strict orders regarding the collection and transportation of gold bullion, jewels, golden Buddhas, ancient religious artefacts, foreign currency, precious metals, and other valuable items, to designated ports, and forward bound to Japan.

The Emperor also posted his cousin, Prince Tsuneyoshi Takeda, to the Kwantung Army staff in Manchuria, and later as his personal liaison officer to the Saigon headquarters of Field Marshall Count Hisaichi Terauchi, to supervise looting and ensure that the proceeds were shipped to Japanese mainland in areas under Terauchi's total control.

He ordered Admiral Masahura, then overall military commander of the Philippines, before General Yamashita and other Admirals and generals, that all war treasure booty taken from the occupied territories of Java, Sumatra, Singapore, Malaysia, Thailand, Burma, Northern India, and the Dutch East Indies be collected and shipped directly to the Philippine Islands when the Americans had blockaded shipping routes to mainland Japan in late 1943.

Although assigned to Saigon, Takeda worked almost exclusively in the Philippines as second in command to Prince Chichibu, Hirohito's brother. Emperor Hirohito named his uncle, Prince Yasuhiko Asaka, deputy commander of the Central China Area Army, in which he commanded the final assault on Nanking, the Chinese capital, between 2nd of December and 6th of December 1937.

The Japanese removed some 6000 tons of gold from Chiang Kai-shek's treasury and many riches from the homes and offices of the leaders of Nationalist China.

By the spring of 1942, the Japanese Imperial forces had captured all South-East Asia, including the Philippines and Indonesia, and the work of "Golden Lily" increased many times over. In addition to the monetary assets of the Dutch, British, French and Americans in their respective colonies, "Golden Lily" operatives absconded with as much of the wealth of the overseas Chinese populations as they could find.

Japanese soldiers tore gold gilt from Buddhist temples, stole solid gold Buddha's from Burma, sold opium to the local populations and collected gemstones from anyone who had any. The gold was then melted down into 75 kg ingots at a big Japanese-run smelter in Ipoh, Malaya and marked with its degree of purity and weight. Prince Chichibu and his staff inventoried all this plunder and put it aboard large merchant ships, usually disguised as hospital ships with large green crosses painted on the side, bound for mainland Japan.

A lot of gold and gems were lost through American Naval submarine warfare, sinking Japanese merchant ships transporting plunder back to Japan. By early 1943, it was only possible for the Japanese to break through the Allied blockade around the main Philippine islands by using submarines. Prince Chichibu moved his headquarters from Singapore to Manila and ordered all treasure shipments from Singapore and Malaya to make their way to Manila, General Santos, Subic Bay, Davao and other "safe" Philippine ports for subsequent reburial.

At the end of the war the Imperial Family's plan was simply to withdraw all their forces from occupied Asia, except the Philippines which would remain under Japanese colonial rule under the banner "Asia for Asians", headed by Judge Jose Laurel as president of a Philippine puppet-type government. This would enable Japan to have a military presence in the country in order to excavate the stolen riches at leisure with little interference from other foreign governments, both near and far. It was always the intention of Emperor Hirohito that all the wealth stored underground in the Philippines would be recovered to only benefit the Imperial Japanese Family who would become immensely rich as a result when the hostilities were over.

There was no plan to share this vast stolen wealth with the Japanese people, indeed it was a plan conceived by greed, and by evil men who would never see this treasure fully recovered in their lifetimes.

General Tomoyuki Yamashita (1885-1946)

General **Yamashita Tomoyuki** was a general of the Imperial Japanese Army.

He was born in a small town called Kochi on the 8th of November 1885. After passing the Cadet's Academy on the 26th June 1906, he attended to the military staff college between 1913 and 1916.

Despite his great ability, he fell into disagreement with the Showa Emperor when he took compassion on the rebel officers of the February 26th incident in 1936.

He also clashed with the Prime Minister, General Tojo Hideki and his supporters. Yamashita insisted that Japan should end the conflict with China and keep peaceful relations with the United States and with the United Kingdom, which earned him an unimportant post in the Kwantung Army.

In 1941 he was placed in the command of the Twenty Fifth Army. In the Malayan campaign, his 30,000 soldiers successfully forced 10,000 British Soldiers in Singapore to surrender. The national Japanese hero was, however, sent to far-away Manchuria again.

In 1944 when the war situation was critical for Japan, when Saipan fell into the American hands in July 1944, Tojo and his cabinet resigned, and a new government was formed. Out of shear desperation, General Yamashita assumed the command of the Fourteenth Army Group to defend the Philippines, replacing Lieutenant General Shigenori Kuroda who was known as a womanizer and liked to drink, he had not contributed significantly to the war effort, and was therefore replaced by a much more able general. General Yamashita arrived in Manila on the 7th of October

1944 with orders to stop the American advance at all cost, or Japan would be the next to fall.

General Mac Arthur and the U.S. army landed on Leyte only ten days after his arrival in Manila. Then the Imperial forces suffered severe defeats in Leyte, where 60,000 Japanese died, out of 200,000 troops who defended the entire archipelago. He tried to rebuild his army but was forced to retreat from Manila to the mountains of northern Luzon.

Japan Surrenders

General Akira Mutō is seen on the left and General Yamashita can be seen on the right of this picture.

The first atomic bomb was dropped on Hiroshima, Japan on the 6th of August 1945, and the second device was dropped on Nagasaki only three days later, because of the terrible devastation these "new atomic weapons" caused. Emperor Hirohito to order a total end to the war on August the 14th 1945 via radio broadcasts to the Japanese nation accepting total surrender. Only in charge for eight short months, General Yamashita was given orders to surrender to the advancing American forces. On the 2nd of September 1945, General Yamashita and his surrender party totaling 21 people surrendered near Kiangan, Northern Luzon to a Major General William H. Gill, then commander of the 32nd Infantry Division, and a special detachment of Company "I" Second Battalion, 128th United States Infantry.

As I stated in my first book the term: "Yamashita's Treasure" was started by President Marcos when he was interviewed by the Cosmopolitan magazine in the late 1970's when he stated that he had found Yamashita's treasure. The treasure never belonged to General Yamashita. The general was in the Philippines ready to defend the Philippines against American and Allied invasion, he was NOT a treasure hunter he was a soldier following orders from his superiors and his Emperor.

I have dowsed so many treasure locations in the Philippines over the past twelve years, and continue to support many treasure hunters both native and foreign looking for Imperial Japanese treasure. I have decided to list some of the GPS locations of where Japanese buried gold is located, awaiting excavation by you the reader.

Dowsed by the Author: 11th September 2011

It is therefore up to reader to further verify my findings using old treasure maps, alive Filipino and Japanese pointers, historical data and seek out known Japanese military buildings and places where Imperial Japanese garrisons
were camped, in order to locate buried hoards of treasure prior to recovery.

The Treasure Hunting Laws are fully described in my first book and how to successfully and legally treasure hunt in the Philippines. Please see the bibliography in the rear pages of this book.

Here is a small listing of the many hundreds of gold locations I have dowsed on the Philippine Islands.

Location	Description	Latitude(North)	Longitude(East)
Bambang, North Luzon.	Imperial Grave Treasure Site 20 Tons.	16°22'58.91"N	121°6'5.92"E
Baguio, North Luzon.	Hospital Treasure Site 3Ton at 35 ft	16°24'07.22"N	120°35'53.99"E
Poro Point, Sual, Pangasinan, N. Luzon.	Imperial Water Treasure Site: Depth:35metres 0.5 Ton	16°04'16.14"N	120°06'47.46"E
Kiangan, N. Luzon.	15-20Kg of small gold bars 6 feet deep.	16°49'19.22"N	121°10'19.72"E
Kiangan, North Luzon.	100kg of small gold bars under road.	16°47'02.01"N	121°07'15.55"E
N. Luzon Teresa 1 (of 4 sites)	Imperial Treasure Site 10 tons of gold bars inside chamber 150 ft	14°33'53.64"N	121°12'4.66"E
North Cebu.	4 tons of small gold bars under a hill 28 feet	11°14'46.15"N	124°02'43.34"E
Escalante City, Mind.	small gold coins 50Kg 15 ft	10°50'27.57"N	123°30'47.70"E
Cavite Manila Bay	Japanese Submarine 4 Ton AU bars	14°28'15.85"N	120°52'24.42"E

29. The Awa Maru Treasure Ship in the Philippines

Awa Maru

The Awa Maru was a Japanese ocean liner owned by **Nippon Yusen Kaisha** Shipping Company. The ship was built in 1941-1943 by Mitsubishi Shipbuilding & Engineering Co. at Nagasaki, Japan. The vessel's pre-war design anticipated passenger service; but when work was completed, the onset of war had created somewhat different priorities.

The ship's name comes in part from the ancient province of Awa on the island of eastern Shikoku in the modern region of Tokoshima. This mid-century *Awa Maru* was the second NYK vessel to bear this name. A turn-of-the-20th-century, 6,309 ton *Awa Maru* was completed in 1899 and she was taken out of service in 1930.

Some background to this particular chapter: When I was researching my first book in 2004, I came across the story regarding the Awa Maru, and rumours that she was carrying a vast cargo of precious metals, jewels and riches stolen by the Japanese Imperial Army during WWII. On the following pages, I explain the history regarding this Japanese merchant vessel and the communications I received from a Filipino treasure hunter from Luzon regarding the fate and location of this famous ship.

History

In 1945 the *Awa Maru* was employed as a Red Cross relief ship, carrying vital supplies to American and Allied prisoners of war (POWs) in Japanese custody. Under the *Relief for POWs* agreement, she was supposed to be given safe passage by Allied forces, and Allied commanders issued orders to that effect.

Having delivered her supplies, the *Awa Maru* took on several hundred stranded merchant marine officers, military personnel, diplomats and civilians in Singapore. In addition, there were stories that the ship carried treasure worth approximately $5 billion USD 40 metric tons of gold, 12 metric tons of platinum (valued at about $58 million) and 150,000 carats (30 kg) of diamonds and other materials such as copper and iron ore. More credible sources identify the likely cargo as nickel babbit and rubber. The ship was observed in Singapore being loaded with a cargo of rice in sacks; however, that evening the dock area where the ship was harboured was reportedly cleared and Japanese troops were brought in to first unload the rice and then re-load her with a new cargo.

Her voyage also corresponded with the last possible location of the fossil remains of Peking Man, which were in Singapore at the time and were, on their own, priceless in value. There are various theories regarding the disappearance of a number of **Peking Man** fossils during World War II. One such theory is that the bones sank with the *Awa Maru* in 1945.

The ship departed Singapore on March 28th, but on April 1st was intercepted late at night in the Taiwan Strait by the American submarine USS *Queenfish* (SS-393), which mistook her for a destroyer. The *Awa Maru* was sailing as a hospital ship under the protection of the Red Cross, and under the agreed rules, she disclosed to the Allies the route she would take back to Japan. Her final route avoided a mine field laid by the Allies.
The four torpedoes fired from the *Queenfish* sank the ship. Only one of the 2,004 passengers and crew, Kantora Shimoda, survived. He was the captain's personal steward, and it was the third time in which he was the sole survivor of a torpedoed ship. The commanding officer of the *Queenfish*, Commander Charles Elliott Loughlin was ordered by Admiral Ernest King to an immediate general court-martial. Commander Loughlin was relieved of command, tried by USN court-martial and convicted of one of three charges, negligence in obeying orders and received a "Letter of Admonition" from the Secretary of the Navy.

As the *Awa Maru* sank "she was carrying a cargo of rubber, lead, tin, and sugar. Seventeen hundred merchant seamen and 80 first-class passengers, all survivors of ship sinking were being transported from Singapore to Japan. The only survivor stated that no Red Cross supplies were aboard, they having been previously unloaded."

This statement would suggest that the orginal cargo of treasure was loaded onto the Awa Maru during the day in rice sacks and then at night taken away and reloaded onto another merchant vessel of a similar size. As you will read later on this chapter this is what I believed happened, and that the ship was sailed from Singapore and deliberately sunk by the Japanese Imperial Army off a small remote island in Northern Luzon in secret.

In the late 1970s, the People's Republic of China began searching for the wreck of the Awa Maru and had successfully located it. Over the course of 3 dive seasons, Chinese divers made 10,000 dives and cleared 10,000 cubic meters of mud from the site. In addition, the Chinese spent $20 million on the *Dalihao*, a specialized salvage barge, to perform marine salvage work on the wreck site.

The Chinese Salvage recovery project of the Awa Maru in the 1980's found nothing of value on the wreck! All they found were human remains (see page 9 of the NSA report link below).

See Link: https://www.nsa.gov/news-features/declassified-documents/cryptologic-spectrum/assets/files/sinkingawa_maru.pdf

According to this CIA (NSA) document the Awa Maru had unloaded its gold cargo in Singapore prior to having "safe passage" back to Japan BEFORE it was sunk by the American submarine, so where did the loot go?

Update

I was approached in 2009 by a Filipino treasure hunter based in Northern Luzon who claimed to know where this ship actually lies, and had proof that the Awa Maru was not sunk by the USS *Queenfish* in 1944. In fact the ship that was sunk could have been the sister ship to the Awa Maru. This ship was similar in size and tonnage she was called the Aki Maru, or was the name placed on another merchant vessel to fool the American Navy? Commander Charles Elliott Loughlin stated that he fired at a silhouette of a large ship so weighed down in the water he believed it to be a Japanese Battleship. This action was taken when the sun was going down in fog. He has no idea of the ships name at the time of the sinking. The ship he sank could have been a Japanese decoy.

The **Aki Maru (shown above)** and **Awa Maru** are sister ships completed in 1942 - 1943. The **Aki Maru** had a Gross Tonnage of 11,409 tons while the **Awa Maru** had a Gross Tonnage of 11,249 tons.

So What Happened To All That Lovely Treasure?

Was it unloaded in Singapore just like the NSA document states, If this was the case then another ship must have been in dock to take the treasure across the South China Sea to a location that was nearer to an Imperial Japanese held Island. It was not possible for ships at the time to sail back to Japan. The US Navy had blockaded the South China Sea. The most logical place to hide a treasure ship would have been the Philippines where thousands of tons of gold and treasure were being buried on the orders of Emperor Hirohito code name "Golden Lily".

Nippon Yusen Kaisha K.K. Shipping Line to Help Divers Identify the Wreck

One of the largest shipping lines in the world, NYK was formed in 1885 by the merger of Mitsubishi Shokai with Kyodo Unyu Kaisha. The company expanded rapidly, initially in the Far East and in 1899 inaugurated a liner service between Japan and London. Later services were expanded to South America, Batavia, Australia, New Zealand, South Africa and western USA and Canada. World War II saw the destruction of much of the NYK fleet and the confiscation of most of the remainder during 1945-46. By the mid 1950's NYK ships were again trading around the world. The advent of popular air travel caused the company to dispose of their passenger ships in the 1960's and to commence establishing container ship routes in 1968. In 1989 NYK revived its passenger ship business with cruise ships and formed the subsidiary Crystal Cruises to handle this operation. The company is still operating today.

Funnel Colours
1885-1929 Black.
1929-1944 Black funnel with wide white band containing two red bands.

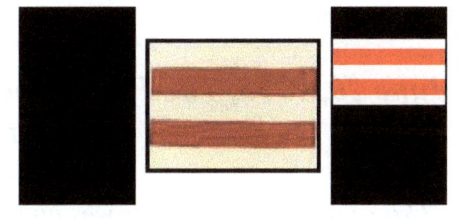

The colour of the funnel can help divers identify a ship wreck so can the ships bell and the name painted on the stern of the ship.

Vessel	Built	Years in Service	Tons
Aki Maru (1)	1903	1934 scrapped Japan.	6,444
Aki Maru (2)	1942	1944 torpedoed and sunk by USS CREVALLE west of Luzon.	11,409
Awa Maru (1)	1899	1930 scrapped Japan.	6,309
Awa Maru (2)	1943	1945 torpedoed and sunk by USS QUEENFISH in Taiwan Strait.	11,249
Chichibu Maru	1930	1934 renamed Tsingtao Maru, 1944 sunk by US air attack off Luzon.	17,498
Eikyu Maru	1944	1944 bombed and sunk at Manila.	6,866

Eiwa Maru	1944	1944 bombed and sunk at Manila.	6,968
Ejiri Maru	1944	1944 torpedoed and sunk by USS LAPON off Luzon.	6,968
Mikasa Maru (1)	1928	1939 sold to Toa Kaiun K.K., Tokyo, 1944 sunk by US air attack in Philippines.	3,143
Suwa Maru (1)	1914	1943 torpedoed and sunk by USS TUNNY, FINBACK and SEADRAGON.	10,927
Shirouma Maru	1944	1944 bombed and sunk off Leyte.	2,858

The above list has been taken from:
http://www.theshipslist.com/ships/lines/nyk.htm#awaji

Clues To The Final Location Of The Awa Maru

Here is an article below from about 15 years ago:

June 20, 1995, The Philippine Daily Inquirer Part 2 of 4 parts.

(This same four part article was on the front page in all six of the other major dailies in the Philippines, including Today, The Manila Bulletin, the Philippine Star, The Daily News, etc.).

Treasures From The Wreck

"APARRI, Cagayan: When Fred Takaki discovered the sunken World War II hospital ship off the coast of Camiguin in 1986 after years of searching, he thought he was found what he was looking for the Awa Maru, believed to be history's richest sunken treasure. The Awa Maru, which sank in the Formosa Strait on April 1, 1945 minutes after it was torpedoed by the US submarine Queenfish, is estimated to be worth between $500 to $5 billion USD.

Takaki, who was born before the war to a Filipina and a Japanese intelligence officer, first heard about a hospital ship loaded with treasures in 1963 from four Japanese friends. They were the ones who got him started on treasure hunting, Takaki says. I was working in Ermita when I met a Japanese friend who needed help to check out a treasure hunting operation in Ipo Dam, Montalban Rizal. They showed me what they got, two Japanese samurais supposedly owned by General Kubota I told him what he was doing was dangerous.

He went back to Japan, Takaki recounts. Several years later, the Japanese returned and invited him to go to Baguio with him to check out some treasure sites. We stayed there for four months. He told me the story of the hospital ship. He said it was in Camiguin in the north. We went to Camiguin and started looking for it. He ran out of money. We never found the ship, Takaki adds. Takaki went back to Camiguin with another group of Japanese who were looking for a "treasure island".

He saw it as his opportunity to look for hospital ship. The ship was loaded I was told with at least 7,000 passengers many of them doctors, nurses, women and children when it was bombed by the Americans.

The story was consistent with what the Japanese told me about the Awa Maru. Only the Awa Maru could have as many passengers, Takaki says. I started scuba diving around the sea. There were a lot of sunken vessels down there, but none seemed to fit the description of the Awa Maru, he says.

Then 1986, Takaki found his ship. Two-thirds of the ship was buried under 30 feet of sand but most of it is still intact.

(The PCJ agreed to withhold the exact location and description of the wreck to protect the interest of the finders.) By this time, Takaki had accumulated some equipment including a metal scanner and a small airlift, which he used to remove the sand from some of the cabins. It was a hospital ship all right. It could not have been a warship because there were no cannons on top or any type of armaments.

A warship does not have as many people in it as this ship. There were laboratories inside medicine containers and hospital equipment, Takaki says. What struck him was the inscription in the keys and the cabin doors were written in English not Japanese, I believed then that I found the Awa Maru, the Awa Maru was of European make, he says. Takaki remove the letters molded in Bronze on the side of the ship and had the Japanese letters translated. The letters read: "Maru" which means ship.

Takaki set out his house in Camiguin to guard his find. He also conducted a small salvage operation on the site of the wreck. This very limited part time salvage effort resulted in the recovery of over 2,000 items, including approximately 800 pieces of Chinese plates, cups, dishes and other ceramics from the Ming, Ching and Sung Dynasties. During the last three years he also recovered 11 small gold bars each one weighing about 100 grams and contained in small wood boxes. He also found dozens of other antiques such as large brass burners, some of them almost 1,000 years old.

Diving for gold Takaki also brought up thousands of bars of tin, brass, lead, zinc, and titanium as well as at least three 62-kilo bags of platinum group metals. Over the years however, Takaki and his native divers using minimal equipment have only manage to skim the surface of the wreck for treasure. Most of it lay underneath sand and metal that was when he decided to look for a financier. He met up with Josue Mapaeg of Nueva Viscaya and Romy Callado of Cagayan, two long time treasure hunters together they looked for a financier who put up the capital needed to salvage all the treasure.

They approached Dennis Standefer bringing with them some of the artefacts that were brought up from the ship. Standefer has been shuttling between the United States and the Philippines buying antiques and artefacts from local dealers and finding a market for them in the United States. He had also worked as a consultant to several treasure hunting projects in the Philippines during the President Marcos and Aquino administrations.

"I get a lot of these stories everyday" he said:" Out of fifty stories you'll be lucky to hear one that isn't pure baloney". They told me about the hospital ship. They showed me artefacts that were 500 to 1,000 years old and supposedly came from the ship. I saw some medical paraphernalia; I heard enough to decide the story was plausible. Standefer stated. He later went back to the United States to carry out more research and to confirm the existence of the Japanese hospital ship that sank in Philippine waters.

He found the documents from the German military and several archives in the United States for which he claim to have paid $10,000. These documents list over 1,000 shipwrecks in the Philippines, and state their exact location and describe their cargo. The hospital ship which sunk in 1945 off Camiguin was one of those listed. Standefer did not state the name of this ship.

The document says it has the biggest treasure on board. Excited, Standefer returned to the Philippines and went to Camiguin to see if the wreck really existed. His team conducted a visual survey of the ship, took videos and photographs of the site and outfitted a 32-foot survey boat. Diving equipment, communications, and a portable computer were transported to the area for survey operations.

Three new compressors were brought to fill scuba tanks used by local divers and to operate the airlifts. Aside from the wreck of the hospital ship, the team also saw the USS Charleston wreck and an additional four ships probably containing treasure. These include another unidentified hospital ship, a third possible treasure carrying Japanese ship, a Spanish galleon with visible brass cannons and an American trading vessel Altogether, the team discovered a total of 33 World War II vintage sunken warship mostly Japanese.

On a clear day most of the wrecks can be seen from the surface, Mapaeg says. The ships are in different states of destruction. There are some, which lie in water less than 100 feet in depth. There are ships lying on top of each other. A lot of them are just a pile of steel. One of them has an airplane sitting on top of it. Standefer says. The team found one hospital ship mostly intact but buried under 30 feet of sand. (The PCIJ agreed not to decide the salvage condition of the shipwreck.) From the location and condition of the hospital ships wreck at least $7 million worth of equipment are needed to salvage the wreck. Standefer estimates, these would include a bigger boat, powerful airlift, underwater cutting torches and metal basket with cranes. Standefer went back the United States to invite foreign investors to bankroll the project.

Meanwhile his Filipino partners formed Pacific SeaQuest, a marine salvage company. In turn, the company signed a contract with Takaki, which give the latter 10 percent of SeaQuests 25 percent share of the find. By law the company is required to give 75 percent of the treasure to the Philippine government. The company applied for and was granted permits to salvage the 33 shipwrecks around Camiguin Island by the Philippine Coast Guard in 1993.

The Office of the President also gave the Pacific SeaQuest the salvage rights to the ships and their cargo including the treasure. One of the shipwrecks with Pacific SeaQuests salvage area is the Charleston. That was when the trouble with Steven Morgan a rival American fortune hunter began."

In 2009 I received an email regarding the real location of the Awa Maru which started me thinking that this could be the final resting place of the ill-fated lost treasure ship. Please read the following pages.

Tue, 31st March, 2009 7:33:40 to: aquila.chrysaetosdavid

"Sir Aquila,

This is Takaki's explanation regarding "The Awa Maru" treasure ship.

A certain Fred Takaki who was then an engineer served as intelligence officer for the Japanese Imperial Army. He married a Filipina, and he stayed here in the Philippines for a long time searching for treasures but stayed in Cordillera area. Until such time we became close to him, and we gained his trust and he was old enough to operate the said sunken vessel on his own. Takaki told me about this ever large haul sunken vessel the "Awa Maru."

"The Japanese Army had **two** Awa Maru ships but only one was declared. The two ships were intended to trick the American battleship in the midway. The one which was not loaded with gold and diamonds served as a decoy which was suicidal in nature for the main purpose was to be hit by the barricade forces in midway so as the other one will slip through. High ranking officials of the Americans already knew about this ship that would carry tons of gold and diamonds to be delivered to Japan but they could not pinpoint which vessel or when it would be delivered.

So it was not an accident as it was told by history, the four torpedoes that was released was an over kill, even two could sink the Awa Maru. But then still the other Awa Maru did not make it through the U.S. barricade it was also hit but the Captain managed to maneuver the ship to a nearby island of Pumuktan, in Camiguin Island north part of Cagayan. Folks in that area even saw this ship. They told us that a ship was docked nearby the island and could be seen by the naked eye. After a week the folks saw the ship had become unbalanced, and later it was gone or had sunk.

A week later fish and sea creatures near the island were seen dying so the local folks were afraid to eat the fish during that time. Takaki even reiterated if the Awa Maru had slipped through the Midway, the war would have continued because the ship contained enough gold and diamonds to supply funds for another year of war with the Allies.

Sir Aquila you might think I am insane right now I am making my own history. Even when I first met this guy I thought he was out of his mind but when we saw the metal marking of the Awa Maru which he had torched from the rear of the ship and the underwater video we were amazed and believed he was telling the truth.

Some local divers are also getting scrap metals from this ship but they cannot get inside the ship since they have just improvised dive equipment and they have no knowledge what was inside the cargo area.

Sir I hope you can find a person who can finance the operation, anyway sir you will have a good share of this even the person who will finance. We will take charge of all the permits here in PI since we still have the permit and the authority to salvage.

Takaki managed to get some of the 6.2Kg gold bars off the wreck, but told me that he needs heavy lifting equipment, a salvage barge and gas cutting equipment to get inside the cargo holds. The wreck he said in lying on the bottom upright but listing to the port side.

Our intention is to salvage the ship and make it a reality since it is already a long year of waiting. Takaki has already died here and yet the ship is still there. Hope Sir you can find the interested person who can help us we will be willing to meet them and have a good deal.

Thank you Sir and more power...."

Island of Pumuktan where I dowsed the gold location of the "Awa Maru" in 2009 in Northern Luzon, The Philippines.

The Awa Maru Location

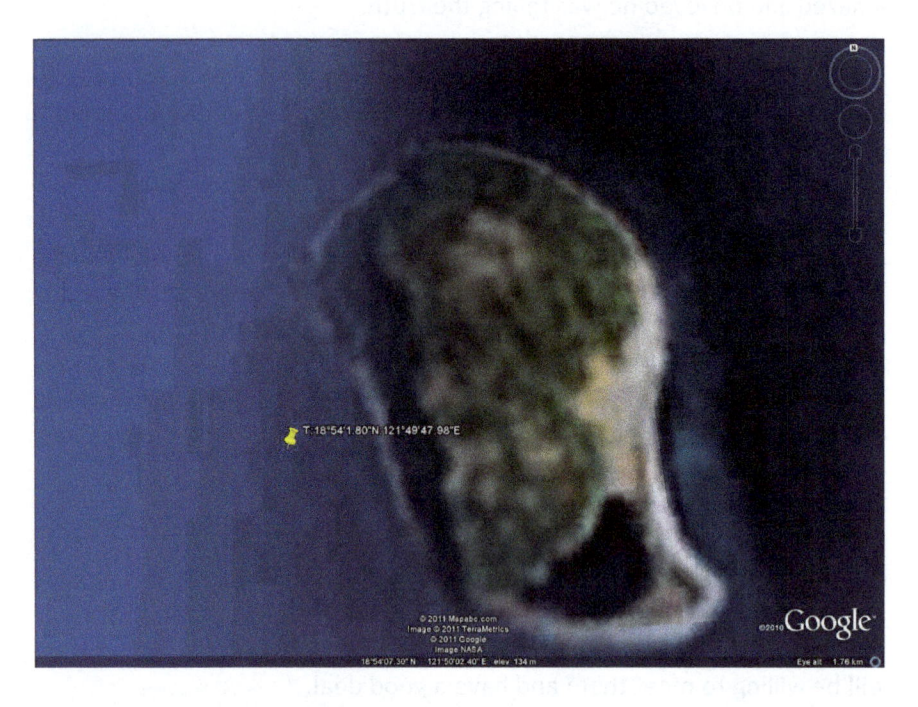

The location of the Awa Maru just off the western side of Island of Pumuktan, Northern Luzon, The Philippines, is an ideal place to deliberately sink a ship laden with treasures due to the isolation of the Island and away from prying eyes.

| Latitude:18°54'1.80"N | Longitude:121°49'47.98"E |

Conclusion

It is not clear whether this ship wreck was ever properly salvaged by Pacific SeaQuest, or indeed any other wreck salvage group. Maybe someone will tell me one day. As I write this I am in contact with a treasure hunting group based near to this Island off Northern Luzon. This group will be travelling to the Island in May 2017 to see if the wreck is still intact awaiting a full treasure recovery.

30. The Flor Do Mar Treasure Ship Location Malacca Straits, Malaysia

The Flor do Mar (Flower of the Sea) was a Portuguese carrack (the largest sailing ship built in its day) that was returning home from the conquest of Malacca. She was already known to be dangerously unseaworthy, but since she was so massive, she was the pride of the Portuguese fleet.

King Alfonso had tasked her with bringing home the vast fortune taken from the King of Siam as tribute. She was caught in a storm in the Straits of Malacca and wrecked on shoals, sinking to rest on the seabed. No one knows exactly where the Flor do Mar lies, and there is some controversy over which country controls the area and wreck salvage rights where she is said to have been lost. Whoever finds this treasure, though, will be the proud owner of over sixty tons of gold and diamonds the size of a man's fist. Well here she is!

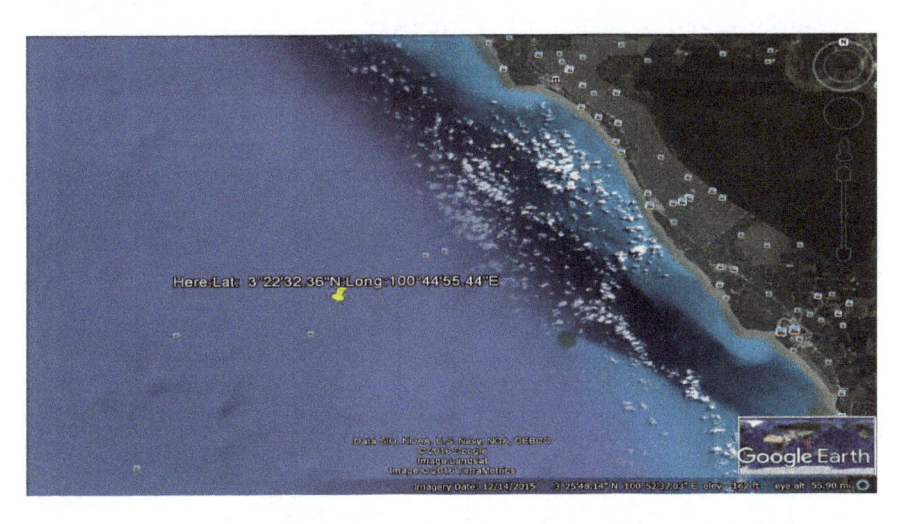

The Wreck lays 27 miles west of Bagan Sungia Tengkorak, Selangor, Malaysia at a depth of 151 feet of seawater and 20 feet under sand. (Dowsed by the Author: 22nd November 2016).

Latitude: 3°22'32.36"N Longitude: 100°44'55.44"E

31. "The Dolphin Wreck" Sri Lanka

Based on historical records there are over 200+ estimated ship wrecks around the coast of Sri Lanka. Many have been located and the search continues to this day using advanced resonance scanning technology for other lost ships. Five hundred years of trade, commerce, conflict and war from the times of the Portuguese, Dutch and the British resulted in vast amount of shipping traffic all around the coast of Sri Lanka and thus the reason for the proportionately high number of wrecks.

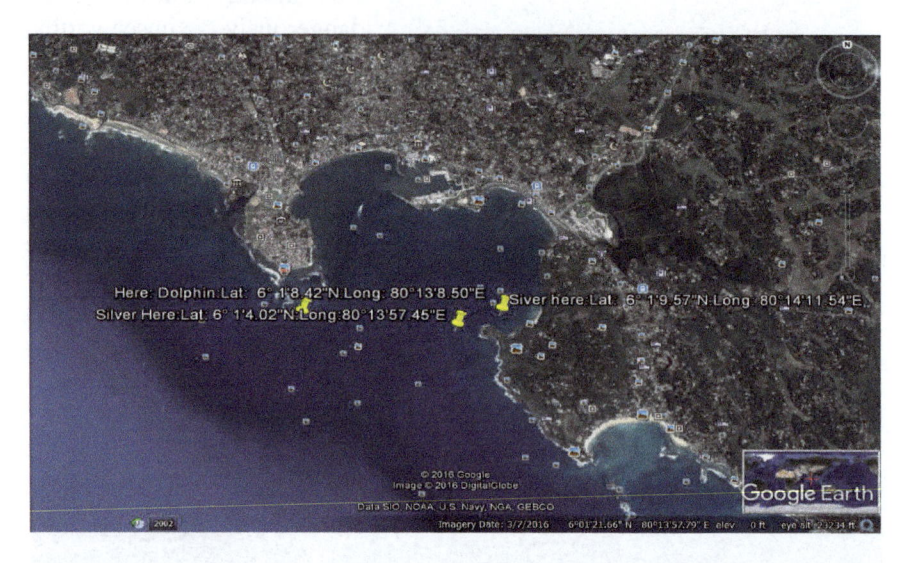

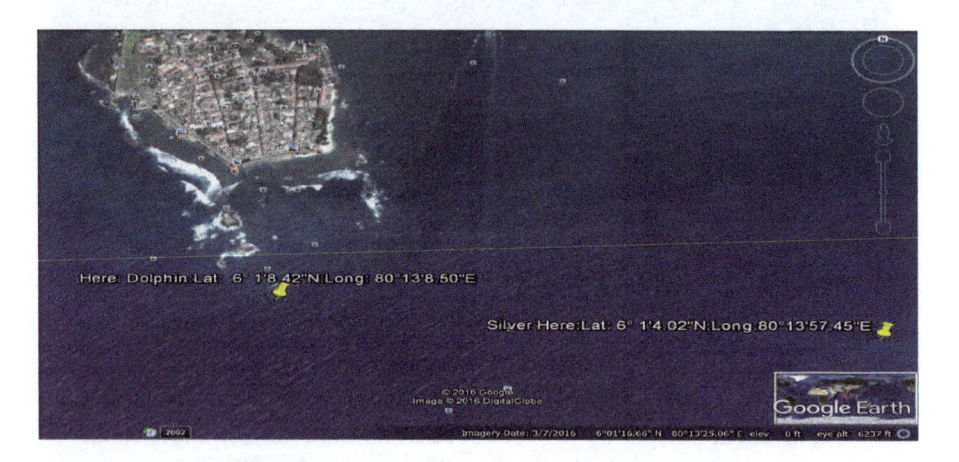

The treasure ship Dolphin wreck is located 578 metres from Der Blick Von Fort on the south shore.

32. Genghis Khan Tomb and Treasure in Mongolia

Genghis Khan was the ruler of the Mongol empire between 1217 and 1227 and created the largest land empire the world had ever seen through bloody battles and conquests made him the richest leader and most powerful man on earth.

During his twenty year reign of war and terror, Khan subdued the Russian princes, his army conquered Persia, Asia Minor, Korea, South-East India, Indonesia, and China.

It is said his treasury contained the combined stolen wealth of China, India and Russia his treasure horde included jeweled Chinese weapons, gold coins from Samark and priceless religious artefacts pillaged from Russian Orthodox churches.

During a campaign against the Chinese, the great Khan suffered a fatal fall from his horse, and in August of 1227 the mourning Mongol army abandoned the conflict to take their leader home to bury him with full military honours he was 65 years of age.

After many months of pomp and ceremony, the body of the fallen ruler was loaded onto a giant ox driven cart which began its long journey towards the Khan's final resting place. Surrounding the cart was a funeral procession 2,500 strong accompanied by a mounted bodyguard of 400 armed soldiers.

Where Is The Body Located?

Many years before his death, Genghis had chosen his own grave site. Stories tell that Khan chose the shelter of a lone tree near the base of Mount Burkhan Khaldun in Mongolia's wild Khingan mountain range. Khan's men dug an elaborate Tomb and Genghis Khan was laid to rest in an ornate coffin. Together went the royal treasure, a massive hoard of gems and precious metals the spoils of war collected by Khan from all the lands he'd conquered in his twenty year reign. Some say the treasure included the crowns of each of the seventy-eight rulers Khan had subjugated, including those of Russia, Persia, and India.

Dead Men Tell No Tales

Legend has it, that Genghis Khan's soldiers killed every person encountered by the funeral procession on its journey into the mountains. And after Khan's body was buried, the soldiers turned their attention to the slaves who dug the tomb, slaughtering all 2,500 of them. When the soldiers returned to Karakorum, Genghis Khan's capital, they in turn were killed by other soldiers so they couldn't reveal the location of Khan's tomb.

To make the Tomb even harder to find, local stories say that a river was diverted over Khan's grave, completely submerging it. Whatever the truth may be, it seems as if Genghis Khan's plan to protect his final resting place was effective. Despite the efforts of many well financed archaeologists and treasure hunters, to this day not one scrap of treasure has been recovered or indeed located.

At Genghis Khan's death, his empire stretched from the Pacific Ocean to the Aral Sea. There are many theories as to where Genghis Khan's final resting place might be. Some say the tomb is within Mongolia's rugged mountains others say he could have been buried in China, where he died during his final campaign.

One of the oldest references to Khan's burial location is the 15th century account of a French Jesuit priest which states that Genghis Khan may have selected as his final resting place, **the confluence of the Kherlen and Bruchi rivers near the Burkhan Khaldun Mountain.** This position does not say how far Khan's burial was from the mountain itself.

This is the area in which Khan was born, and according to the French priest, after a major military victory, Khan reportedly said that this place would be forever his favourite

The Herlen River is still known today, but attempts to locate the "Bruchi" River have drawn a blank and the river is unknown to modern day cartographers. Unfortunately this makes it impossible to pinpoint the exact location for the tomb specified in the ancient texts.

Amateur archeologist, Maury Kravitz, who's been obsessed with Khan's tomb for forty years, did discover a toponym "Baruun Bruch" ("West Bruch") in the area roughly 100 km east of Burkhan Khaldun
(48° N 110° E).

In 2004 he conducted excavations there to no avail. So, the location of Khan's tomb and the vast treasure it may contain remains one of archaeology's greatest unsolved mysteries, until now. I dowsed the area on the 1st of January 2017, and below are my findings. You will see that my co ordinates are south west of Amateur archeologist, Maury Kravitz, excavations some 44 miles away.

Above we can see my dowsed location of where Khan is buried and where Maury Kravitz carried out his excavations in 2004.

Dowsed by the Author: 1st January 2017

Latitude: 47°33'44.68"N Longitude: 109°19'15.07"E

Here we can see that this point is very close to where two ancient rivers once met. There is a river valley where once two rivers meet in a Y shaped formation. (4 Tons of treasure here).

In geography, a confluence is the meeting of two or more bodies of water. Also known as a *conflux* it refers either to the point where a tributary joins a larger river, called the main stem, or where two streams meet to become the source of a river. This I believe to be the lost river Bruchi that flowed into a tributary of the Herlen river close by in 1227 when the rivers would have been fast flowing and known to Genghis Khan as the rivers of life.

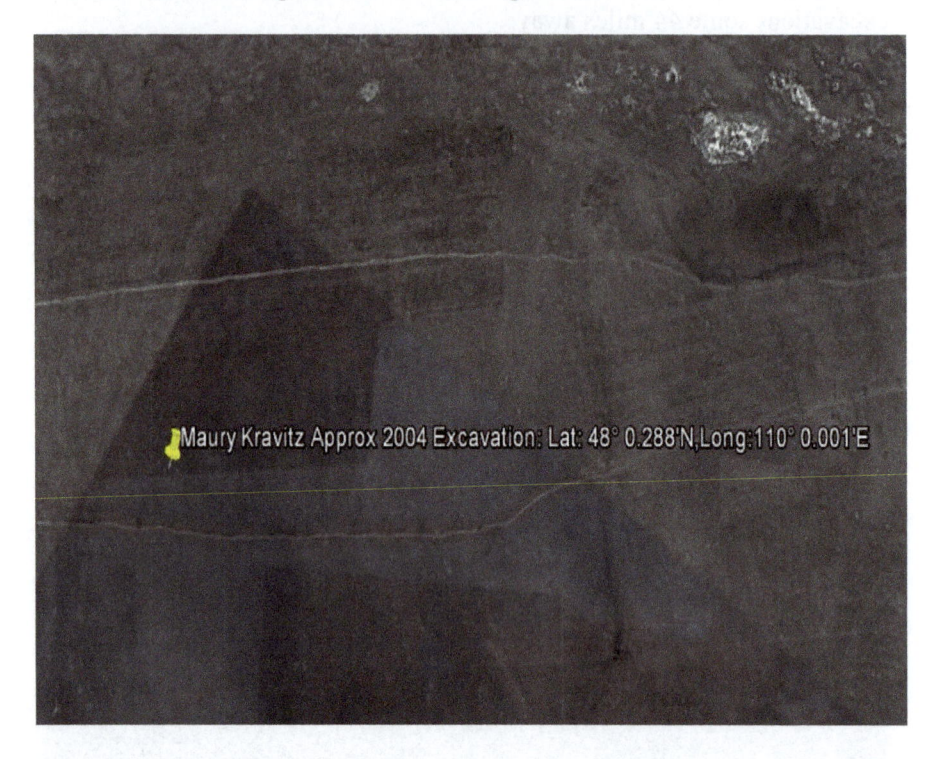

Maury Kravitz Approx 2004 Excavation: Lat: 48° 0.288'N, Long: 110° 0.001'E

Above we can see from this picture there is no evidence of rivers meeting here or a vast dense forest. Kravitz proved that this was not Khan's burial site in 2004. Another treasure expedition will now have to be launched in order to verify my findings. The use of Lidar and Infrared satellite technology and Ariel Magnetometer surveying techniques would help in locating the last resting place of the infamous Genghis Khan and his hidden treasure.

33. Red Sea Treasure Ship Wrecks Egypt

In 1996 I learned to scuba dive with Emperor Scuba School based at Hurghada, Red Sea Egypt. As a bit if fun I decided to see if I could dowse locations of any gold carrying ships that have been lost in the Red Sea since the last great wars of 1914-18 and 1939-45.
In this chapter I have included all of the ship wreck locations I have dowsed just for their gold content and given you the reader the GPS locations of where they now lie.

These two ship wrecks are off the west coast Of Saudi Arabia, One is Greek merchant ship and the other an old American Liberty ship captured by the Germans during WWII.

1945: Greek Ship Ran aground Laying upright: American Liberty ship Artefacts stolen from Egypt and Israel: 100 Tons of Au combined.

Dowsed by Author:
7th November 2007.

T1:125 feet deep.
T2: 98 feet deep.

Target 1 Location: Latitude: 25°48'53.22"N Longitude: 36°28'27.23"E

Target 2 Location: Latitude: 25°45'55.51"N Longitude: 36°30'43.12"E

34. The Ancient City of Tanis Treasure Location Egypt (Modern Sân el-Hagar.)

The city of Tanis is relatively unknown among Egypt's wealth of historical sites, though it yielded one of the greatest archeological troves ever found. Once the capital of all Egypt, Tanis's royal tombs have yielded artefacts on par with the treasures of Tutankhamun.

The treasures found in the "lost city" of Tanis rival those of King Tut's. Yet for more than six decades the riches from its rulers' tombs have remained largely unknown.

A City Vanishes

Tanis was known by many names. Ancient Egyptians called it Djanet, and the Old Testament refers to the site as Zoan. Today it's called Sân el-Hagar.

The site, in the Nile Delta northeast of Cairo, was capital of the 21st and 22nd dynasties, during the reign of the Tanite kings in Egypt's Third Intermediate period.

The city's advantageous location enabled it to become a wealthy commercial center long before the rise of Alexandria. But political fortunes shifted, and so did the river's waters, and in recent centuries the Tanis site had became a silted plain with some hill-like mounds thought to be of little interest.

It was known that the ancient city was hidden somewhere in the area, but not where.

"People kept trying to identify different places with it," said Salima Ikram, a professor of Egyptology at American University in Cairo and a National Geographic Society grantee stated.

Egypt's "intermediate periods" were times of weak central government when power was divided and sometimes passed out of Egyptian hands. During this time the rulers of Tanis were of Libyan decent, not scions of traditional Egyptian families. That distinction may have contributed to the city's disappearance in later years.

In 1939 a French archaeologist named Mr Pierre Montet brought Tanis into the 20th century after nearly 11 years of excavations. He unearthed a royal tomb complex that included three intact and undisturbed burial chambers and the tombs held dazzling funeral treasures such as golden masks, coffins of silver, and elaborate sarcophagi. Other precious items included bracelets, necklaces, pendants, tableware, and amulets.

One of the kings, Sheshonq II, was unknown before Montet discovered his burial chamber. But he wore elaborate jewelry that once adorned the more famous Sheshonq I, who is mentioned in the Bible. Sheshonq I was a pharaoh of ancient Egypt and the founder of the twenty-second Dynasty.

"That shows you that *the kings of Tanis* were very important at least during that time period," Silverman said.

Tanis was found largely as it was abandoned, so the city is home to many archaeological treasures in addition to the tombs. Temples, including a Temple of Amun and a Temple of Horus, have been found. Even urban districts of the ancient city remain, and the site continues to host archaeological expeditions in search of more finds. The Au Target is located at:

Latitude: 30°58'47.72"N and Longitude: 31°53'11.69"E

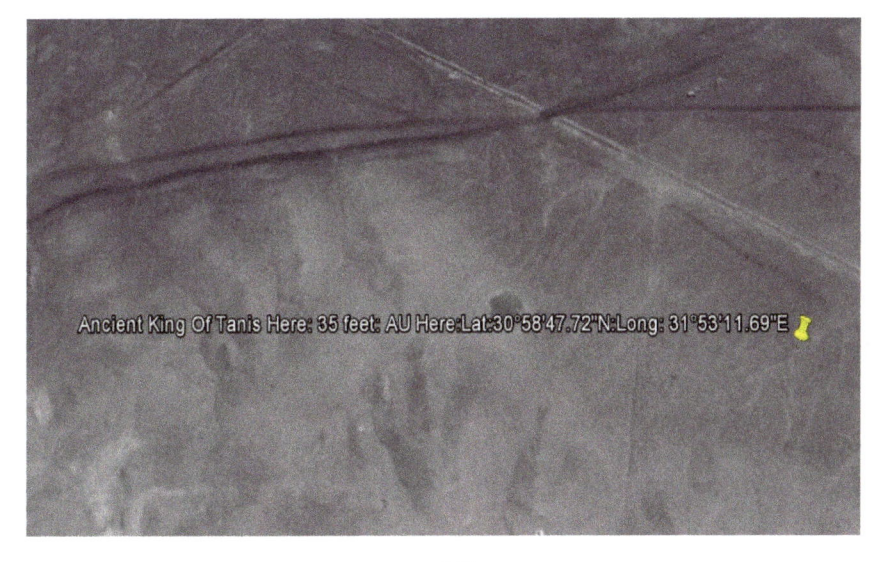

35. The Treasure Locations on Cocos Island

Just 350 miles west of Costa Rica you will find the tiny and uninhabited Cocos Island. It is believed that a vast treasure was hidden here in 1821 by the mutinous crew of the *Mary Dear* (or *Mary Deare,* depending on source), a British ship chartered to move gold, silver and jewels from the churches of Lima, Peru to the safety of Spain.

Legends say that the Great Treasure of Lima, consisting of eleven boatloads in all, were buried there by pirate called Thompson of the brigantine **Mary Dear** in 1821-22 in a cave with a natural door. This natural door may be part of a cliff that revolves or a door that can be wedged with rocks.

Shortly after leaving the port of Callao, the crew of the Mary Dear murdered the six soldiers charged with guarding the treasure, seized control of ship and sailed to Cocos Island where, it is said, they hid the treasure in a cave and then set sail for Panama.

Arriving in Panama the mutineers were arrested, most of the crew executed, but three were spared after promising the Spanish authorities that they would assist in the recovery of the hidden treasure. Two of the three were taken to Cocos by a detachment of soldiers, soon after arriving, the two men escaped from their captors into the dense jungle. The soldiers, unable to locate the mutineers and believing that the two men would be unable to escape the island, returned to Panama.

A year later, the two men were picked up by a passing ship and taken to Costa Rica. One of the two mutineers passed on the location of the treasure, in the form of a map, to a man named Mr John Keating. Keating, with the help of the third man named Boag later located the treasure on the island but the crew of the ship that had taken them to Cocos and demanded a share, facing a mutiny, Keating and Boag hid in the jungle until the crew gave up searching for them and sailed away.

Pirate Treasure Island

Benito Bonito, the Portuguese pirate also used this island to bury his millions in 1820. Pirate William Dampier is also said to have excavated several caves in the sandstone in 1822 and hidden treasure valued at over $60 million. The captain of the wrecked vessel Lark is supposed to have taken $72,000 to the island and buried it.

Efforts to trace these treasures including the crew of the schooner *Fanny* in 1871 found nothing. A Captain Welch also tried in 1871 with the same result. Schooner *Vanderbilt* tried again in 1879 with no luck. In all, over 450 expeditions have set out to locate the treasures, all have failed.

After an unknown period, Keating was picked up from the island by a passing ship and claimed that Boag had drowned, although he would later state that he had murdered him and left his body in the cave with the treasure horde.

Before his death in 1882, Keating passed the Cocos treasure secret on to three people his wife, Mr Fred Hackett and Mr Nicholas Fitzgerald. Why he did not go back for the bulk of the treasure himself is not clear.

Keating's widow and Fred Hackett teamed up and headed to Cocos, they found nothing. The third man, Nicholas Fitzgerald, did not go in search of the treasure but passed the map Keating had given him to Admiral Henry Palliser, who came away empty handed.

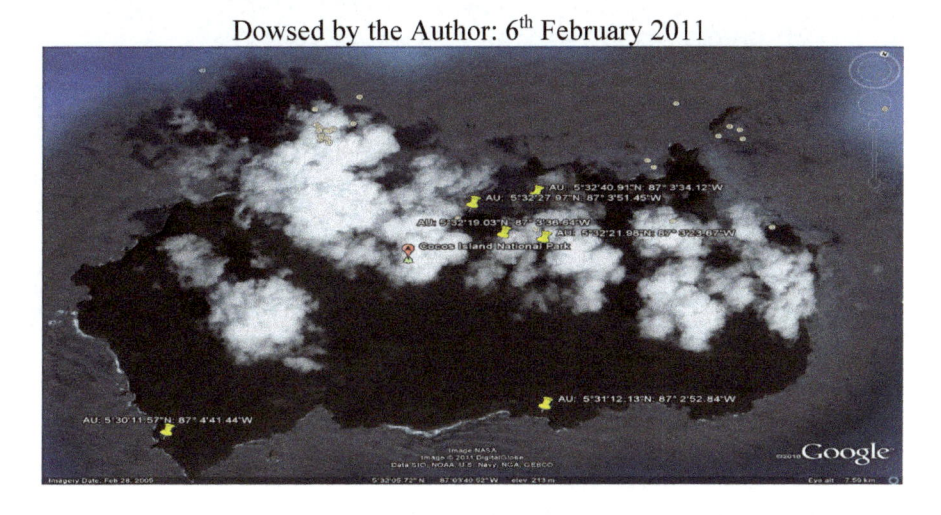

Dowsed by the Author: 6th February 2011

Latitude N	Longitude W
AU Here: 5°31'12.13"	87°02'52.84" 15 feet deep in sand
AU Here: 5°32'40.91"	87°03'34.12" 32 feet deep in sand
AU Here: 5°33'27.97"	87°03'51.45" 22 feet deep in sand
AU Here: 5°32'19.03"	87°03'36.46" 18 feet deep in cave
AU Here: 5°32'21.98"	87°03'23.67" 25 feet deep in hole
AU Here: 5°30'11.57"	87°04'41.44" 38 feet deep in cave

36. Island Of Dominica Spanish Fleet Location

In 1567 six vessels of a Spanish fleet were wrecked on the Northwest tip of the Island of Dominica. It is said that they carried over 3 million in gold pesos, and that the survivors were captured and eaten by the Carib Indians. During a salvage attempt a year later it was learned that the local Indians had salvaged the treasure and hid it in caves. They would not say where, even under threat of death. There are no records of the treasure ever being found.

Dowsed by the Author: 1st January 2017

Gold Buried 8 Boxes Here:
Latitude: 15°37'651"N Longitude: 61°27'607"W

Spanish Ship Wreck Latitude: 15°38'002"N Longitude: 61°28'101"W

The gold pesos are buried in a small valley south of Capuchin inside a cave some 15 feet beneath the ground. The area is covered by trees and overgrown jungle. There are several chests of gold coins and silver buried in this location awaiting somebody to recover them.

The Spanish shipwreck some 0.67 miles from the buried treasure horde also contains gold pesos coins but not so much as the cave treasure.

37. Conclusion

The word **Treasure** from the Greek language Θησαυρός -meaning "treasure store" is a concentration of riches, often those that originate from ancient history and considered lost and hidden to humanity until being rediscovered once again by you.

In this book I have given you, the treasure hunter and adventurer, past history and in-depth knowledge of where to look for buried treasure, and just maybe you will decide to become a successful dowser yourself. Everyone has the ability to become a successful dowser all it takes is practice and an open mind.

Your independent research is crucial in sifting out fact from fiction. This book has taken me over twelve years of research and dowsing maps of the world. Now it is your turn to run your race for the hidden treasure.

My second book is not supposed to be the "definitive answer" to all the unanswered questions that you may come across regarding your site analysis and treasure recovery activities, but I hope that it will aid you in finding answers and ultimately result in you successfully recovering a small amount of the billions of dollars worth of buried gold, gems and artefacts still awaiting to be discovered, whether sunk or buried around our great planet earth.

May your God bless you and keep you safe and happy treasure hunting, now go and live the dream, because life is very short indeed.

Aquila.

Bibliography

The Successful Treasure Hunter's Essential Dowsing Manual by David Villanueva: Published by True Treasure Books **ISBN 0-9550325-0-4** (www.truetreasurebooks.com).

Successful Treasure Hunter's Secret Manual: Discovering Treasure Auras in the Digital Age by David Villanueva **ISBN 978-0-9550325-5-4** (www.truetreasurebooks.com)

General Yamashita's Dream Book: How To Successfully Find Treasure In The Philippines by Aquila Chrysaetos **ISBN 978-1-909740-29-7** (www.Amazon.com)

Uri Geller's Crystal Pendulum Dowsing Kit: Find Wealth, Health and Well-Being by Dowsing and Divining, Uri Geller **ISBN 978-1842931943** Watkins Publishing

Van Der Molen, S. J. (1970) *The Lutine Treasure* **(ISBN 0-229-97482-1)**

Elizabeth Brown Dowsing: The Ultimate Guide for the 21st Century **(ISBN 978-1848502208)**

Appendix

Concrete Breaking Solutions: (Non Explosive Demolition Agent)

Bristar, Address: BASF Philippines, Inc.11/F Hanjinphil Corporation Building 1128 University Parkway, North Bonifacio, Global City, Taguig, Metro Manila, 1634, Philippines. E-Mail **lie.chico@basf.com** Phone (63-2) 811 – 8000 (63-2) 811 – 8000 Telefax: (63-2) 838 - 1025

Bristar: (non-explosive demolition agent) (more or less 2,000 pesos per 5 kg/bag) Address: Condeck Sales Center, Room 201, Torimar Bldg, 370 Escolta St. Sta. Cruz, Manila, Philippines. Tel: (632) 2425647 / 2418201 1269 Makati City Phone +63 2 845 29 81Telefax: +63 2 845 29 93

Ter-Mite (Non Explosive Demolition Agent)
Dextec Oy Ltd.
Otsolahdentie 7
FI- 02110 Espoo
Finland
Fax +358 9 8565 7261
Website link:
http://www.ter-mite.com/?gclid=CPCi1raFia8CFQITfAodNWCt-Q#

Dexpan Non Explosive Blasting:

Website link: http://www.dexpan.com
How to use Dexpan video:
http://www.youtube.com/watch?v=YlDQvgM4pKM&feature=related

Concrete Dissolving Solutions:

Molecular Cement Dissolver: Website link:
http://www.romixchem.com/romix_cart/back_set.php
Muriatic Acid for Concrete Etching: Website link:
http://www.nycoproducts.com/products.asp?pid=81

Concrete Cutting Solutions:

Core Drilling:
www.coredrillcity.co.uk/masonry.php?osCsid=b269um62q432dvdutle1thd4t2

Petrol Disc Cutters: www.tooled-up.com/Product.asp?PID=143003

Diamond Drill Bits: Concrete and marble:
www.discountdiamondbits.com/3prosecobit.html

Gold Prices:

www.metalprices.com/FreeSite/metals/gold/gold.asp
www.goldprice.org/
www.cooksongold.com/metalprices/
www.livecharts.co.uk/MarketCharts/gold.php
www.taxfreegold.co.uk/goldpriceslive.html

Ground-Penetrating Radar and Electromagnetic Induction Instruments

Applications
- Wells
- Cellars
- Secret Tunnels
- Hidden Rooms
- Buried or Hidden Objects
- Cemetery Surveys
- Aircraft Wreckage
- Can be used in a boat to locate sunken vessels or vehicles
- See through walls to locate hidden rooms or voids
- Locate and Identify ferrous and non ferrous
- Finds Gold and Silver

See:
Geophysical: www.geophysical.com
Geofizz: www.geofizz.co.uk/p
Geomatrix: www.geomatrix.co.uk

Internet Treasure News Groups:

www.treasurenet.com
www.THunting.com
www.ukdetectornet.co.uk
alt.treasure.hunting
www.tseatc.com/ww2loot.html

Metal Detector Manufactures:

Accurate Locators: www.accuratelocators.com
Deep Search (Gold Scan 5 metres) Metal Detectors
http://ktselectronic.com
Fitzgerald Detectors: www.treasurenow.com
Search and Recovery Service:
www.treasurenow.com/html/SearchAndRecovery.html
Garrett Metal Detectors: www.garrett.com
Metal Detector Sales: www.kellycodetectors.com
Minelab International Ltd: www.minelab.com
OKM 3D Image Gold Detectors:
www.okmmetaldetectors.com/index.php?lang=en#
Whites Electronics (UK) Ltd: www.whites.co.uk

Long Range Metal Detectors:

Rangertell Long Range Detectors:www.rangertell.com/indexcc.htm
Electroscope Long Range Detectors: www.electroscopes.com/
www.okmmetaldetectors.com/index.php?lang=en#

UNITED INTERNATIONAL GROUP
Website : www.uigdetectors.com
Email : uigdetectors@gmail.com
OKM: http://www.okmmetaldetectors.com/products/longrange/bionic-x4.php?lang=en

Lidar and Magnetometer Aerial Surveys:

http://sgl.com/services.html

Salvage Grab:

SMIT Salvage
P.O. Box 59052
3008 PB Rotterdam
The Netherlands. Phone + 31 10 4549911 Fax + 31 10 4115095
Email: salvage@smit.com   Website: www.smit.com

Thermal Image Cameras:

www.thethermalimagingcamera.com
www.isgthermalsystems.co.uk

Underwater Cutting Equipment:

www.broco-rankin.com/broco/underwater.cfm

Useful Contacts:

Casio "Pro Trek" Sports Watches: www.casio.com
Colorado Gold Dowsing Sticks: www.coloradogoldsticks.com
DENR (Philippine treasure permits): www.denr.gov.ph
Gas Masks And Ventilation Systems: www.scottint.com
Sarin Gas Detectors: http://www.detcon.com/xgas-sarin01.htm
Methane Gas Detectors: http://www.detcon.com/xgas-methane01.htm
Hydrogen Cyanide Detectors: http://www.detcon.com/xgas-hydrogencyanide01.htm
Mustard Gas Detectors: http://www.detcon.com/xgas-mustard01.htm
If you are not sure of the Karat content of the gold, purchase an M24 Stock# TES-170.00: This device will assay gold ranging from 9-24-Karat.

GPS Units:

www.garmin.com
http://www.magellangps.com/

Laser Thermometres:

www.testersandtools.com/Infrared-Laser-Thermometer.php

Dowser Contact Groups:

American Society of Dowsers
http://dowsers.org/
British Society of Dowsers
https://www.britishdowsers.org/http://www.healthdowsers.org/about.htm
Keith Harmon: Programme Co-ordinator International Association of Health Dowsers (IAHD) 52 Helen Avenue Feltham Middlesex TW14 9LB Tel: 0208 751 0417
Canadian Society of Dowsers:
http://canadiandowsers.org/
Guernsey Society of Dowsers:
http://guernseydowsers.co.uk/index.html
International Dowsing Groups:
https://www.britishdowsers.org/affiliated-groups/international/